Marlene Creates

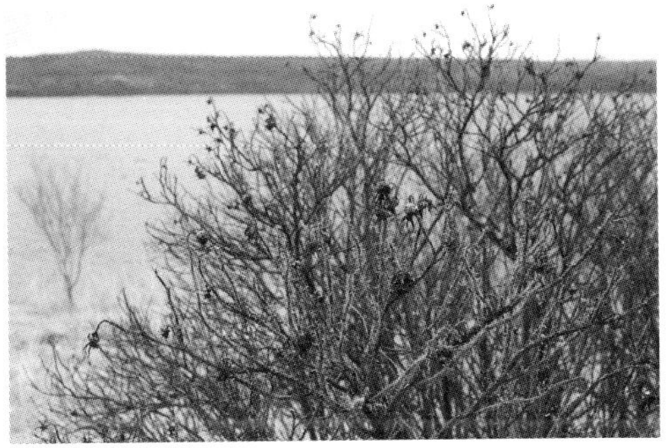

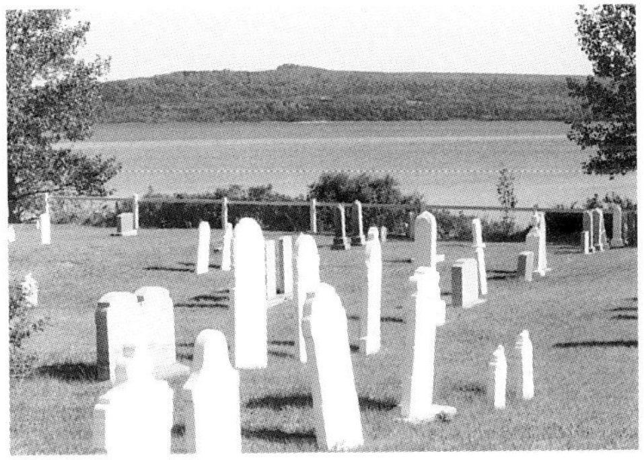

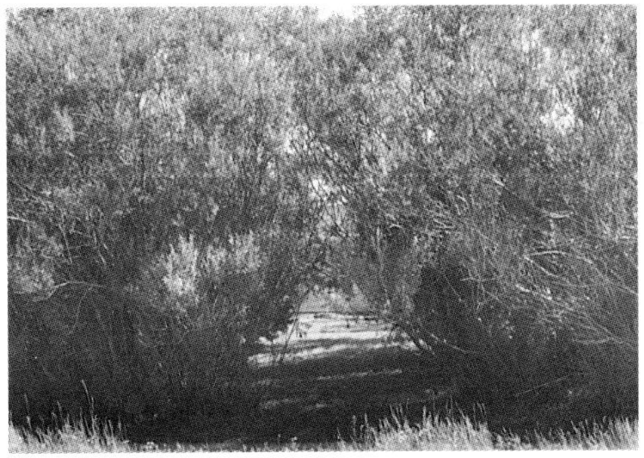

Places of Presence:

Newfoundland kin and ancestral land,

Newfoundland 1989-1991

THE CANADA COUNCIL FOR THE ARTS SINCE 1957 | LE CONSEIL DES ARTS DU CANADA DEPUIS 1957

We acknowledge the support of the Canada Council for the Arts for our publishing program.

Marlene Creates acknowledges the assistance of The Canada Council for the Arts and the Newfoundland & Labrador Arts Council for assistance in the production of this work during 1989-1991.

This publication is A Year of the Arts 1997 Project, partially sponsored by the Department of Canadian Heritage, NewTel, Nortel, and Tele-Direct Atlantic.

Printed on acid-free paper

Photography: Marlene Creates, except installation views and photographs of natural objects: Ned Pratt.

Design: Beth Oberholtzer

Published by: KILLICK PRESS
a Creative Publishers imprint
a division of 10366 Newfoundland Limited
a Robinson-Blackmore Printing & Publishing associated company
P.O. Box 8660, St. John's, Newfoundland A1B 3T7

Printed in Canada by: ROBINSON-BLACKMORE PRINTING & PUBLISHING

Canadian Cataloguing in Publication Data

Creates, Marlene.
Places of presence.
ISBN 1-895387-87-6

1. Creates, Marlene – Exhibitions. 2. Newfoundland – In art – Exhibitions. I. Title.

N6549. C74A4 1997 709'.2 C97-950149-0

ARTIST'S STATEMENT

PLACES OF PRESENCE:

Newfoundland kin and ancestral land, Newfoundland 1989-1991

This series focuses on a set of hand-drawn memory maps and spoken texts in which my relatives in Newfoundland express memories about themselves and the land on which they were born. Several have moved away; many have lived in the same place their whole lives. The series concentrates on three precise bits of "landscape": the places where my grandmother, my grandfather, and my great-grandmother were born.

These narratives and memory maps are accompanied by photographs of my relatives and of the landmarks I was directed to by their stories. I took the photographs of the places to rhyme with the memory maps they drew for me. The series also includes my own memory maps and stories of my experiences as a visitor to my ancestors' land. I also collected natural "souvenirs" there, including stones, leaves, and seaweed.

The series reveals a pattern of land use in rural Newfoundland where land has been passed down from generation to generation, divided into smaller and smaller pieces among sons and nephews and, with some interesting exceptions, inherited by daughters. But the statements that interest me most are the ones I regard as poetic and even elegiac – describing an affectionate connection to the places and a sadness over changes and loss that have occurred over time. This may be seen as sentimental. I believe, though, that this is not merely of nostalgic interest, although I do this work, every part of it, with my heart pounding in my chest. When I listen to stories of my family's history in Newfoundland (which I've never heard before), I sense that these stories come from a past that affects me. When I walk around the land, when I choose the stones from the shore, when I look at my notes and photographs, I feel a poetic inheritance that cuts across me as a woman and as an artist. These intersections are powerful, some are painful, and all are elusive, fragile, and improbable. But I have no difficulty in stating the central premises of my present work. I have tried to reflect on the natural environment, spatial relations, land use, and geographical imagination.

This series of stories and photographs is like a net that was set at one point in the flow of people, events, and natural changes that make up the history of these three places. I see these places as palimpsests, as impressed with those people and events as the surface of an old slate blackboard or a marked wooden table-top. When we describe the land – or, more frequently, remember events that occurred at particular points on it – the natural landscape becomes a centre of meaning, and its geographical features are constituted in relation to our experiences on it. The land is not an abstract physical location but a *place*, charged with personal significance, shaping the images we have of ourselves.

Marlene Creates, 1991

CONSTITUTING *PLACES OF PRESENCE*:

Landscape, Identity and the Geographical Imagination

CONSTITUTING *PLACES OF PRESENCE*:

Landscape, Identity and the Geographical Imagination

Joan M. Schwartz

"When we describe the land – or, more frequently, remember events that occurred at particular points on it – the natural landscape becomes a centre of meaning, and its geographical features are constituted in relation to our experiences on it."[1]

With this simple, but eloquent statement, Marlene Creates situates her work as a visual artist within the fabric of contemporary inquiry into representation, memory, landscape, meaning, culture and identity. In *Places of Presence: Newfoundland kin and ancestral land, Newfoundland 1989-1991*, Marlene Creates sets out to reflect upon "the natural environment, spatial relations, land use, and geographical imagination."[2] While these four concerns establish the touchstones of her work, Creates' exploration is more conceptual than topographical, more emotional than mathematical. She is concerned with many things and, ultimately, goes beyond the natural environment as a physical entity, beyond spatial relations as a cartographic exercise and beyond land use in any practical or economic sense. Creates does not simply describe the land of her ancestors or define the experience of place in Newfoundland or distil the cultural essence of Newfoundland "folk" or celebrate the simpler life of earlier times[3]. Rather, weaving all these concerns into a rich tapestry of land and life, Creates gives visual expression to the complex workings of the geographical imagination. In *Places of Presence* land is transformed into landscape, and space becomes place as ancestral land is invested with meaning by the experiences and memories of her Newfoundland kin. In turn, Creates recognizes that her own identity is inextricably linked to place.

Creates' "reflections" take the form of three assemblages depicting the land where her grandmother, her grandfather and her great-grandmother were born. Each assemblage comprises a series of clusters; each cluster consists of a photographic portrait, a memory map, a transcribed narrative, and a landmark photograph; some include a found object. The portrait of an individual posed comfortably in personal domestic space identifies the relative who drew the memory map and related the adjacent story. Creates has taken care to transcribe each narrative to preserve the storytelling quality of oral family traditions. The narratives were elicited by the drawing of the memory maps which, in return, give them depth. In them are expressions of experiences that constitute the meaning of place. "Landmarks" are not collective or publicly recognized, but rather idiosyncratic and highly personalized: the damson tree, the aspens, the old currant bushes, the big old apple tree, the old house, great-grandmother Tamar's flower garden, a huge rock, a swinging gate, a woodpile, a well. The found objects which Creates includes in her assemblages – aspen leaves, kelp, beach stones, birch logs – are "repositories of place-based meaning."[4] Unlike the other elements in each cluster, they bear a connection to place with a different ontological basis. They are not representations of places of presence, but rather physical fragments which contain the "presence" of place. The found objects, each referred to in a narrative, supply the fine details and material textures that, for Creates, define the distinctive elements of and give material expression to her spiritual connection to the ancestral land of her Newfoundland kin. Creates' own narrative as a participant observer introduces each assemblage; there, her own memories mingle with those of her Newfoundland kin.

With a creative eye, she tackles the complex interactions between landscape, memory and identity, deftly integrating a range of scholarly issues. In *Places of Presence*, Creates explores, at a visual, conceptual, and almost visceral level, the way in which experience constitutes landscape meaning, and landscape meaning anchors identity. Separately and collectively, the assemblages and clusters help us to visualize the relationship of people to place, and to understand the constructedness of landscape and identity. Through carefully crafted and internally cohesive groupings of words, images and objects, Creates explores the territory where landscape, memory and identity converge. Each cluster presents, simultaneously, four or five points of access by which to enter the relationship between the artist's Newfoundland kin and ancestral land. In them, the contours of the geographical imagination find artistic expression. Past links to present, place to space, identity to landscape. In the slippages between past material reality and remembered lived experience are the imagined communities, invented traditions, performative memories and cartographic illusions of the geographical imagination.[5]

CONSTITUTING PLACE

"To experience a geographical place, ... is to want to communicate about it."[6]

What is it that Creates, with the assistance of her Newfoundland kin, wants to communicate about ancestral land? *Places of Presence* does not fall into geographical description; it does not attempt to tell us what certain places look like now nor how they got that way. The maps are neither detailed nor accurate. The spatial relations they communicate are more idiosyncratic than cartographic. The maps reveal more about dynamics than distances, more about the geographical imagination than topographical reality, more about identity than genealogy, more about the character of memory than the nature of land.

Creates' exploration of landscape as "a centre of meaning" penetrates to the heart of current scholarly inquiry into representation and the ways in which perceptions of place and place-based identity are generated, negotiated, confirmed and contested. In particular, *Places of Presence* addresses questions with which geographers have long struggled: how do we identify, think about, experience, and attach meaning to landscape?[7] Creates, herself, engages in many conventional fieldwork practices: she walks about on the land, draws maps, conducts interviews, takes photographs, collects specimens, and records memories, but the result of her work is not geography. Nor, for that matter, is it sociology or history. Creates' work transgresses and transcends disciplinary boundaries. In *Places of Presence,* Creates' work as a visual artist acts as a conduit through which to explore and express the relationship between landscape and experience. Concern to validate Creates' work as art or to valorize it as more than "just sociology or anthropology"[8] can be unproductive and misleading. For Creates, the "contest of meaning" is played out across the visual and verbal spaces of her assemblages. Unencumbered by jargon, devoid of pretension, her arguments are straightforward and immediately accessible; her interpretation of the geographical imagination through artistic expression helps the viewer visualize the critical connections and complex issues associated with living in, responding to, and understanding places.

PLACE AND MEMORY

> *"The notion of sense of place would be impossible without memory, the recollection of personal history grounded in a particular landscape or set of landscapes.... Anything that awakens such memories or keeps them alive – ... can be understood as an expression of the sense of place."*[9]

Places of Presence is very much about memory – places of memory and memories of places. It is not local history or family history, but a cumulative remembrance of times, places and things past. It demonstrates that, "Memory is life, ... always a phenomenon of the present, a bond tying us to the eternal present.... It thrives on vague, telescoping reminiscences, on hazy general impressions or specific symbolic details."[10] Eva Moore (née Freake) remembers a

Lewisporte that was "beautiful, quiet, serene." Her sense of place flows, not from the Lewisporte of the new housing development, but from memories of a Lewisporte that no longer exists, of open spaces and of skating on the harbour by moonlight. Nellie Decker (née Freake) declares, "Look, if we didn't have our memories we wouldn't have much, would we.... Nothing left there now. Memories is all.... It's not the same anymore." Moore and Decker express nostalgia in the literal sense of "loss of home" through either physical or temporal displacement. But, as Pierre Nora has observed, memory "is rooted in the concrete: in space, gesture, image, and object."[11] *Places of Presence* employs space, gesture, image and object to recover memory and define place, to constitute landscape and unravel identity.

The memory maps which form the nucleus of each cluster and the focus of each narrative, are not so much about space on the ground as place in the mind. Joan Freake pictures everything as being square, admitting that her memory map is rooted in "a child's conception" of the land. Carl Layte warns that his map is rough, drawn freehand from memory and not to scale. Freake and Layte apologize for the lack of precision in their maps. Embedded in their apologies is the common expectation that maps are supposed to be accurate depictions of spatial relations and topographical features. But the cartographic inaccuracies, discrepancies and inconsistencies within and between maps of the same plot of land in Lewisporte or in Joe Batt's Arm take the viewer beyond issues of topography, land use and inheritance. In them, the filter of memory and the lens of time only serve to colour and magnify the differences between responses to the same landscape and reveals more about human experience than spatial relations. The memory maps are not descriptions of the land as much as cartographic expressions of sense of place, mediated by, reinforced by and shaped by memory. Different maps of the same land demonstrate Creates' point that different people experience and remember physical space in different ways. Here, in the plurivocality of place, Creates' Newfoundland kin speak to us – though not necessarily in unison – about ancestral land, the "palimpsests" where her grandmother, grandfather and great-grandmother were born.

EXPERIENCE AND MEANING

"Place is created when experience charges landscape with meaning."[12]

Late twentieth-century scholarship critiques mimesis and privileges meaning. Landscapes are no longer "anything and everything seen from the top of a hill."[13] Rather, they are, "constructs of the imagination projected onto wood and water and rock."[14] Landscapes emerge from "the interplay between the observer, on the one hand, and the landform and land use on the other."[15] Creates' relatives construct meaning for the landscapes of Lewisporte and Joe Batt's Arm through their individual memories and through the collective memories of family and community. Experience imparts meaning; presence makes place; landscape confers identity. *Places of Presence* carries the notion that "human use confers meaning on space" from the macro level of society to the micro level of individuals in a family. Her assemblages serve as sites where, in the contest between reality and representation, meaning is acquired, negotiated, constructed, preserved and communicated.

In many ways, *Places of Presence* overcomes the "uncertainty about adequate means of describing social reality" brought about by the crisis of representation in the human and social sciences.[16] Over the last decade, all forms of representation as well as notions of reality, truth and authority have been problematized. The notion of reading landscapes as "text" has found favour because it addresses "the inherent instability of meaning, fragmentation or absence of integrity, lack of authorial control, polyvocality and irresolvable social contradictions that often characterize them...."[17] However, as W.J.T. Mitchell has suggested, we need to think of "landscape" not as a noun, but as a verb, and to ask, not what it is or what it means, but what it does. For Mitchell, landscape is not "an object to be seen or a text to be read, but ... a process by which social and subjective identities are formed."[18] *Places of Presence* demonstrates the processes by which place acquires meaning. It anchors memory and shapes identity. It weaves family land and family history into the texture of Newfoundland life and demonstrates the intimate and intricate connections between landscape, memory and identity which Creates calls her poetic inheritance.

LANDSCAPE, IDENTITY AND THE GEOGRAPHICAL IMAGINATION

"The land is not an abstract physical location but a place*, charged with personal significance, shaping the images we have of ourselves."*[19]

Places of Presence is about Newfoundland, its landscapes and Creates' kin; but, above all, it is about Creates and the discovery of her own place-based sense of identity. In his monumental work, *Les Lieux de Mémoire*, Pierre Nora contends: "A world that once contained our ancestors has become a world in which our relation to what made us is merely contingent."[20] Not so for Marlene Creates. *Places of Presence* explores a relationship between Creates and the world that contained her ancestors – the places where her grandmother and grandfather and great-grandmother were born – that is not contingent but causal. Creates is profoundly affected by the "affectionate connection" to ancestral land expressed by her Newfoundland kin. From each assemblage emerges a genealogical and a geographical sense of place, a "poetic inheritance" which grounds Creates' own identity. Creates' exploration of the birthplaces of her Newfoundland kin is a search for her own identity and the way it is constituted through ancestral land and family memory.

Places of Presence is very much a journey of self-discovery for Creates. Emerging from the clusters and assemblages are "places of presence" where Creates finds her own placed-based identity as a woman and as an artist. She picks her way along the wild and rocky shore of the land where her grandfather was born, thinking about the people who walked there before. She strolls with her mother over the land where her grandmother was born, thinking about the four generations of women the land has passed to. She camps on the land where her great-grandmother was born, tracing her roots to the fishing stages and flakes of Joe Batt's Arm. In the process of listening to stories, looking at the memory maps, taking photographs, and collecting found objects, she finds a past that grounds her sense of place and identity in ancestral land and Newfoundland kin.

Ultimately, *Places of Presence* is more than an exploration of the artist's ties to family and place. In the attention she draws to the slippages between land and landscape, between space and place, between memory and history, we find lessons for understanding the processes that link the material to the symbolic, past to present, nature to culture, people to place. Situated against scholarly inquiry into landscape, memory and identity, Creates' assemblages can be seen to embody and clarify some of the concepts and tensions underlying the creation and use of public space, social memory and national identity. Creates' conclusion that experience charges landscapes with personal significance and that our sense of place serves to shape the images we have of ourselves can be projected onto issues of regional or national identity, literature and iconography at levels beyond. *Places of Presence* expresses the idea that symbolic landscapes are "part of the shared ideas and memories and feelings which bind a people together."[21] In it, cartographic, photographic, literary and physical representations combine to demonstrate how landscapes are experienced, remembered and invested with meaning. Creates gives artistic expression to the geographical imagination. What emerges are visual insights into the enduring relationship of people to place.

Acknowledgements: The research and writing of this paper was supported by Education Leave from the National Archives of Canada, a Doctoral Fellowship from the Social Sciences and Humanities Research Council of Canada, and the Year of the Arts 1997, sponsored by the Department of Canadian Heritage and NewTel. I extend my thanks to Brian Osborne for his many insights into the meaning of landscape and the nature of memory, to Lilly Koltun and Terry Cook for their careful reading of the manuscript, and to Marlene Creates for her enthusiasm and encouragement, patience and friendship.

Joan M. Schwartz is Chief of the Photography Acquisition and Research section of the National Archives of Canada, and a Social Sciences and Humanities Research Council of Canada Doctoral Fellow in the Department of Geography, Queen's University, Kingston, Ontario.

1 Marlene Creates, "Artist's statement," *Places of Presence: Newfoundland kin and ancestral land, Newfoundland 1989-1991*, 1991.
2 Creates, "Artist's statement," *Places of Presence.* In her previous exploration of the relationship between landscape and experience in the series *The Distance Between Two Points is Measured in Memories*, Creates was concerned with the dualism of environment and society – what is experienced as nature and what is experienced as culture.
3 Ian McKay, *The Quest of the Folk: Antimodernism and Cultural Selection in Twentieth-Century Nova Scotia.* Montreal and Kingston: McGill-Queen's University Press, 1994.
4 Kent C. Ryden, *Mapping the Invisible Landscape: Folklore, Writing, and the Sense of Place.* Iowa City: University of Iowa Press, 1993, p.75.
5 Benedict Anderson, *Imagined Communities: Reflections on the Origin and Spread of Nationalism.* rev. ed., London: Verso, 1991; Eric Hobsbawm and Terence Ranger (eds.), *The Invention of Tradition.* Cambridge: Cambridge University Press, 1983; Paul Connerton, *How Societies Remember.* Cambridge and New York: Cambridge University Press, 1989; J. B. Harley, "Historical geography and the cartographic illusion," *Journal of Historical Geography*, 15, 1, 1989, pp.80-91.
6 Ryden, *Mapping the Invisible Landscape*, p.19.
7 See, for example: Kay Anderson and Fay Gale (eds.), *Inventing Places.* Melbourne: Longman Cheshire, 1992; Michael Bunce, *The Countryside Ideal: Anglo-American Images of Landscape.* London and New York: Routledge, 1994; James Duncan and David Ley (eds.), *Place/Culture/Representation.* London and New York: Routledge, 1993; J. Nicholas Entrikin, *The Betweenness of Place: Towards a Geography of Modernity.* London: Macmillan, 1991; Peter Jackson, *Maps of Meaning.* London and New York: Routledge, 1992; John Rennie Short, *Imagined Country: Society, Culture and Environment.* London and New York: Routledge, 1991; Yi-Fu Tuan, *Space and Place: The Perspective of Experience.* London: Arnold, 1977.
8 In a review of the group show, "Margins of Memory," at the Art Gallery of Windsor, Gary Michael Dault expressed concern that "something has to make it art rather than just sociology or anthropology." (*Canadian Art*, Spring 1994, p.67). In a more perceptive interpretation, Susan Gibson Garvey suggests that it is Creates' "careful and precise aesthetic judgement that enables us to read these pieces as *art* rather than sociology." ("The Specificity of Place," *Marlene Creates: Landworks 1979-1991.* St. John's: Art Gallery, Memorial University of Newfoundland, 1993, p.23).
9. Ryden, *Mapping the Invisible Landscape*, p.75.
10 Pierre Nora, "General Introduction: Between Memory and History," *Realms of Memory: Rethinking the French Past.* Volume I: Conflicts and Divisions. English-language Edition edited and with a Foreword by Lawrence D. Kritzman. trans. Arthur Goldhammer. New York: Columbia University Press, 1996, p.3.
11 *Ibid.*
12 Ryden, *Mapping the Invisible Landscape*, p.221.
13 John Taylor, "The alphabetic universe: photography and the picturesque landscape," in Simon Pugh (ed.), *Reading Landscape: city – country – capital*, Manchester: Manchester University Press, 1990, p.177.
14 Simon Schama, *Landscape and Memory.* Toronto: Random House, 1995, p.61.
15 Kenneth H. Craik, "Psychological reflections on landscape," in Edmund C. Penning-Rowsell and David Lowenthal (eds.), *Landscape Meanings and Values*: report of a symposium organised by the Landscape Research Group and held on 4-6 April 1984 at the Royal Institution, London, and Down Hall, Essex. London: Allen and Unwin, 1986, p.48.
16 George E. Marcus and Michael M.J.Fischer, "A Crisis of Representation in the Human Sciences," *Anthropology as Cultural Critique: An Experimental Moment in the Human Sciences*, Chicago and London: The University of Chicago Press, 1986, p.8.
17 Trevor J. Barnes and James S. Duncan, "Introduction," in Trevor J. Barnes and James S. Duncan (eds.), *Writing Worlds: discourse, text and metaphor in the representation of landscape.* London and New York: Routledge, 1992, p.7.
18 W.J.T. Mitchell, "Introduction," in W.J.T.Mitchell (ed.), *Landscape and Power.* Chicago and London: The University of Chicago Press, 1994, p.1.
19 Creates, "Artist's statement," *Places of Presence.*
20 Nora, *Realms of Memory*, p.7.
21 D.W.Meinig, "Symbolic Landscape: Some Idealizations of American Communities," in D.W.Meinig (ed.), *The Interpretation of Ordinary Landscapes: Geographical Essays.* New York and Oxford: Oxford University Press, 1979, p.164. The notion is developed in a Canadian context by Brian S. Osborne, "The iconography of nationhood in Canadian art," in Denis Cosgrove and Stephen Daniels (eds.), *The Iconography of Landscape: Essays on the symbolic representation, design and use of past environments.* Cambridge: Cambridge University Press, 1988, pp.277-312.

PLACES OF PRESENCE:

Newfoundland kin and ancestral land, Newfoundland 1989-1991

where my grandmother was born

from the series ***Places of Presence: Newfoundland kin and ancestral land, Newfoundland 1989-1991***

assemblage of:
13 black & white photographs, selenium-toned silver prints, each 8 x 10 in. (20 x 25 cm) framed,
1 colour photograph, cibachrome print, 8 x 10 in. (20 x 25 cm) framed,
6 memory map drawings, pencil on paper, each 8.5 x 11 in. (22 x 28 cm), framed 11 x 14 in. (28 x 36 cm),
6 story panels and 1 title panel, screen print on plexi, each 11 x 14 in. (28 x 36 cm) framed,
aspen leaves, framed 16 x 20 in. (41 x 51 cm),
beach stone,
wooden shelf, 20 feet long x 7.25 in.deep (6 m x 18 cm).

installed dimensions: 63.5 in. high x 21.5 feet long x 7.25 in. deep (161 cm high x 6.5 m long x 18 cm deep), plus floor space.

where my grandmother was born

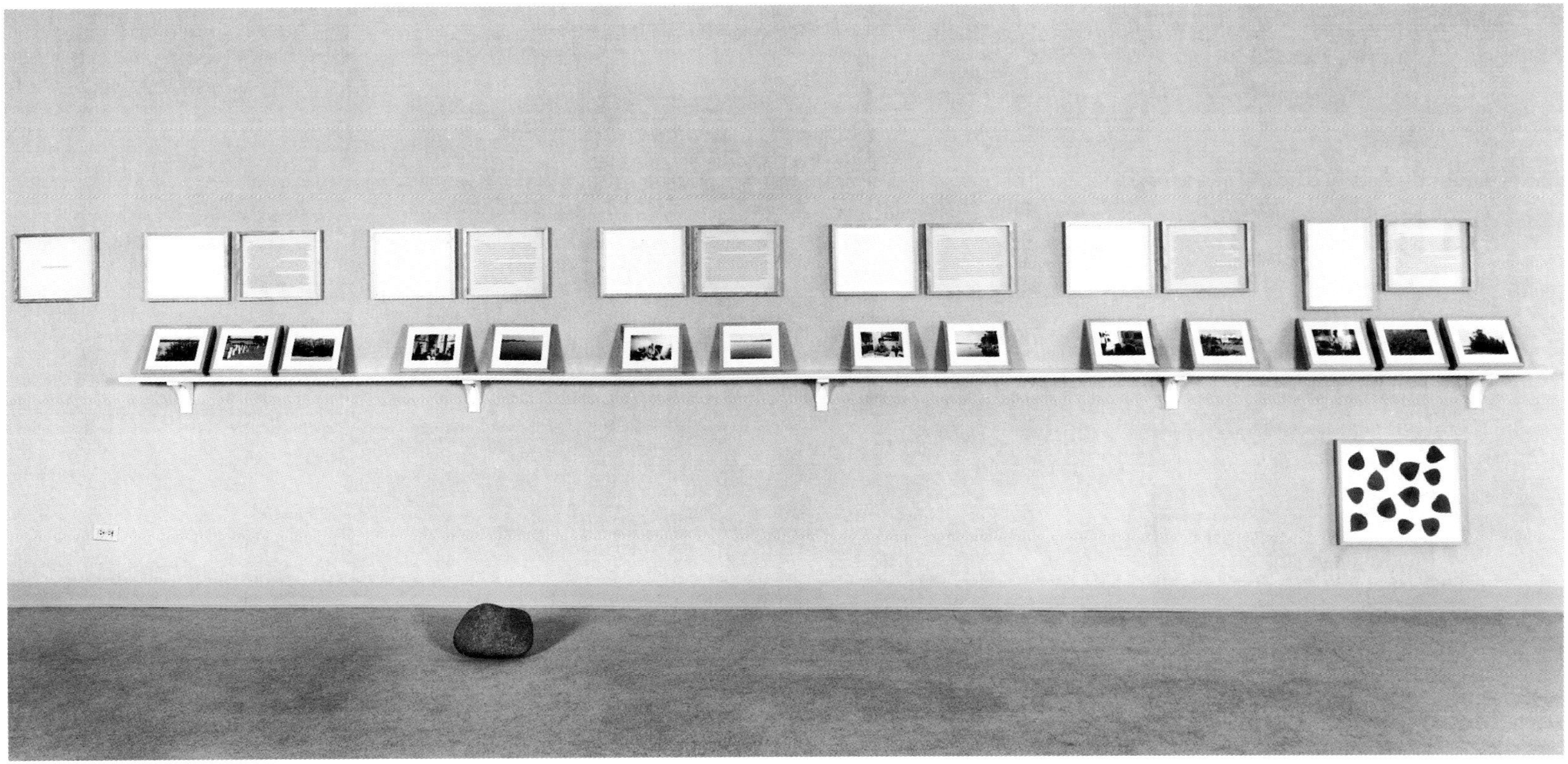

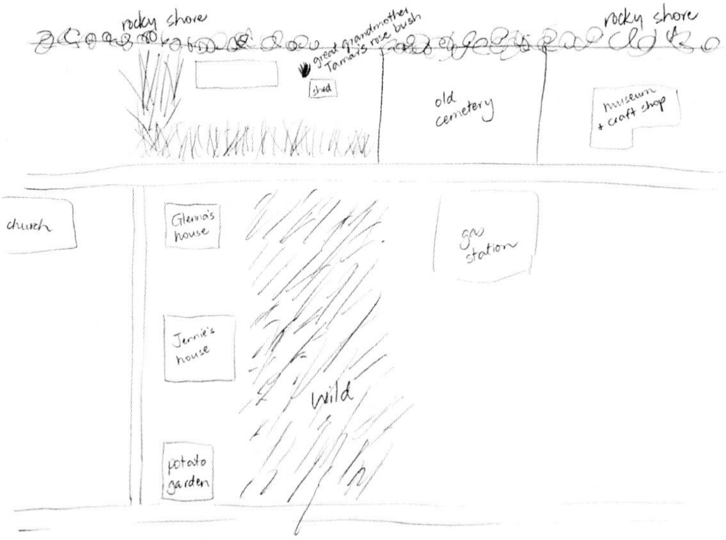

My memories

The first time I went to Newfoundland was 1981 and it was Easter weekend. I took my mother with me and I had my twenty-ninth birthday when I was there. We stayed at Jennie's house. Jennie's house is on the land that came from her mother, Melinda, and Aunt Melinda got the land from her mother, that's my great-grandmother Tamar. And Tamar got the land from her parents. And now Glenna, that's Jennie's daughter, has built her house on the same land again, right in front of her mother's house. That's four generations of women that the land has passed to. I remember that the property on the water side of the road was really grown over, full of big high bushes all grown up, and the house that was there had been boarded up. And there was a little shed. Anyway, Jennie and Mom and I walked across the road and walked around over on that side. Jennie pointed out that the old rosebush beside the shed, that was still alive, had been her grandmother's rosebush, my great-grandmother Tamar's rosebush. And I took a picture of it because of that.

Mom and I also, just the two of us, walked around the old cemetery. The cemetery is between the two places: it's between where my grandmother was born and where my grandfather was born. In other words, my grandfather married the girl next door, only for the cemetery in between the two places, where the ancestors of both of them were buried. I remember that Mom was particularly moved standing in front of her grandparents' graves. That would be Tamar and Nathaniel Turner, my great-grandparents. I think she was sad because she'd never known her grandparents, because her parents left Newfoundland after her older sister was born and they moved to Toronto, where my mother was born. And they never returned, that is, her parents never came back, not even for a visit. So my mother never went to Newfoundland either, until she was, well, my mother must have been in her fifties the first time she ever went to Newfoundland.

When the last daughter of Tamar and Nathaniel died, the land on the water side of the road was left for years and years with nobody knowing exactly who it belonged to, although there was Jennie who had always lived there and all this land had belonged to her grandparents at one time. Now the land over on the water side has since been sold by a public auction. And the person that bought that land has tidied the place up a bit. But there's a lot of big high bushes left, so that from the road it still looks pretty hidden. And I don't know if the rosebush is still there because I haven't been able to see it, either from the cemetery or from the road. It's a very strange feeling that the land where my great-grandparents lived and where my grandmother was born now belongs to strangers, and it feels like a forbidden place where I can't go anymore. When I collected the leaves from my great-grandparents' big old aspen trees, I felt like I was trespassing.

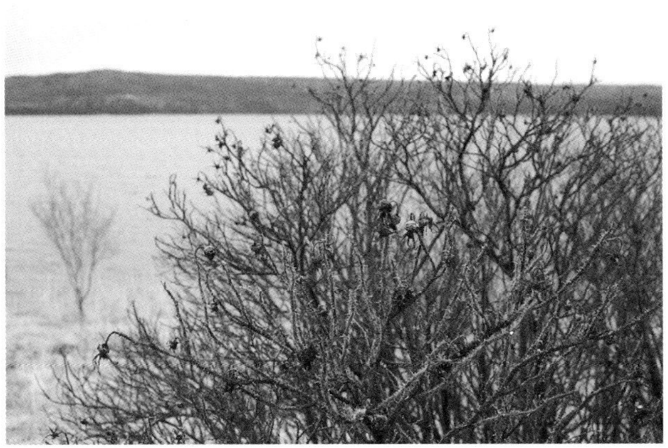
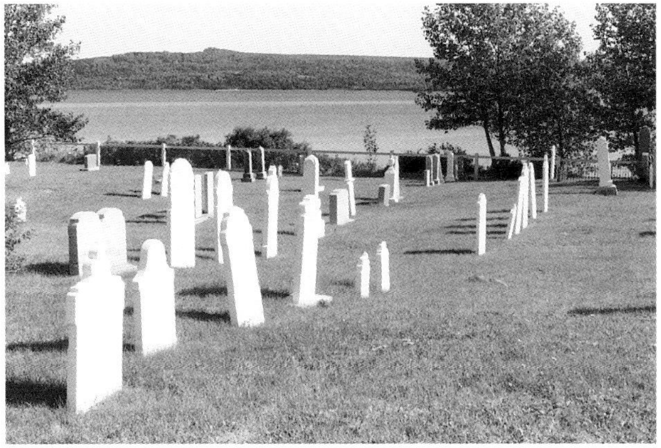
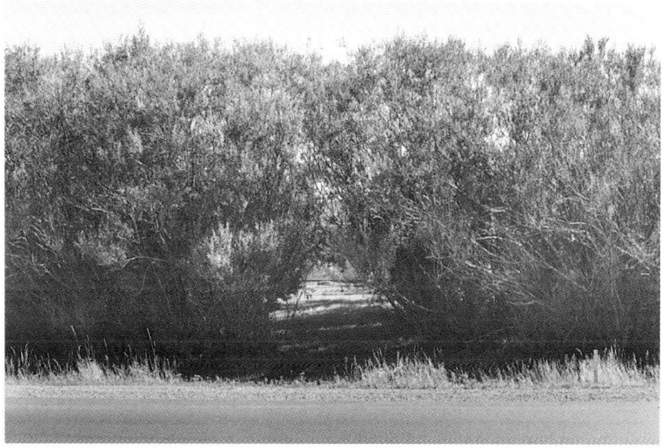

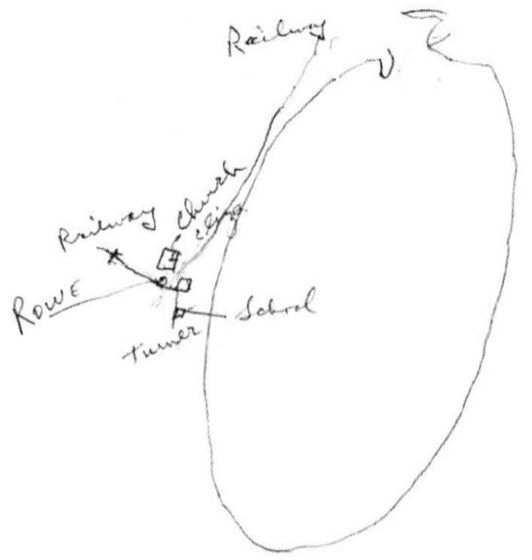

Fred Rowe

This would roughly be Lewisporte. That's the entrance, that's what makes Lewisporte one of the best harbours in Newfoundland. That would be the church. It is on my grandfather's, your great-great-grandfather's, land. When they had to build a new church, my grandfather James sold the land for fifty dollars. His brother was down here too. His name was Elijah. Originally there were three brothers: James, Elijah, and John Freake. John stayed in Joe Batt's Arm. Our family lived here, right next to the church. And now just look at this, Turners on the water side of the road and we were on the other side. James gave his daughter, Aunt Tamar, and Uncle Nat Turner an excellent stretch of land running right from the water, running right in over the railroad track, right into the country.

Uncle Nat, for most of his life, he was a ship's pilot. Lewisporte was a shipping harbour. Large ships had to come into Lewisporte. About twenty miles outside they would pick up a pilot and he would guide the ship. This story was that Uncle Nat, your great-grandfather, was taking a ship through a very difficult passage with a lot of rocks, visible and invisible. And the captain of the ship would be a European, probably Norwegian. Norwegian ships used to bring the coal to Lewisporte for the trains to burn. Lewisporte was the end of the branch. This captain was getting a bit nervous and he said to Uncle Nat, "Pilot, do you know where all the rocks are around here?" And Uncle Nat said, "No captain, I don't. I'm afraid I don't." And the captain got a little bit more worried, "What are you doing bringing the ship in through all these rocks?" And Uncle Nat said, "I don't know where all the rocks are, but I know where there aren't any."

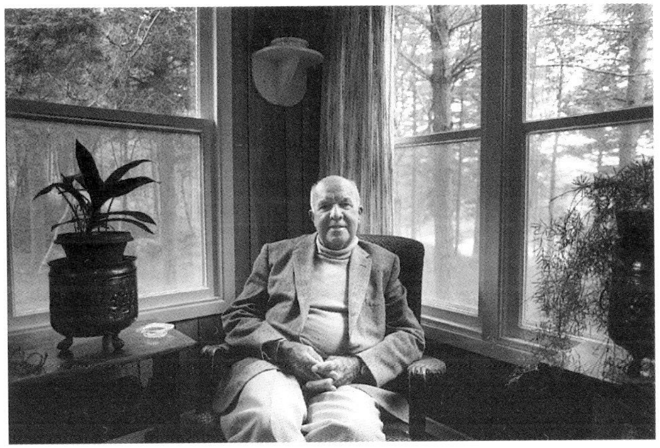

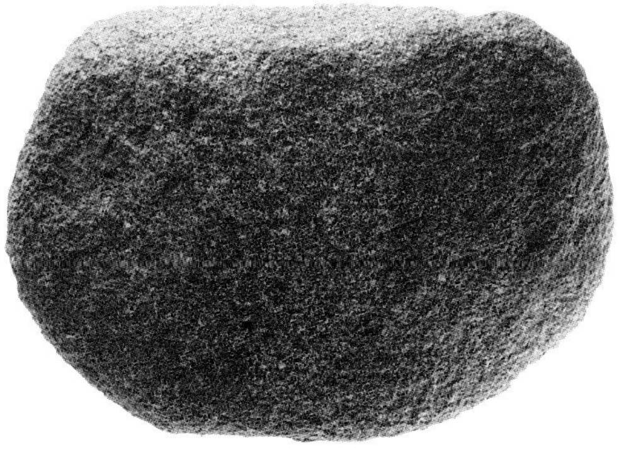

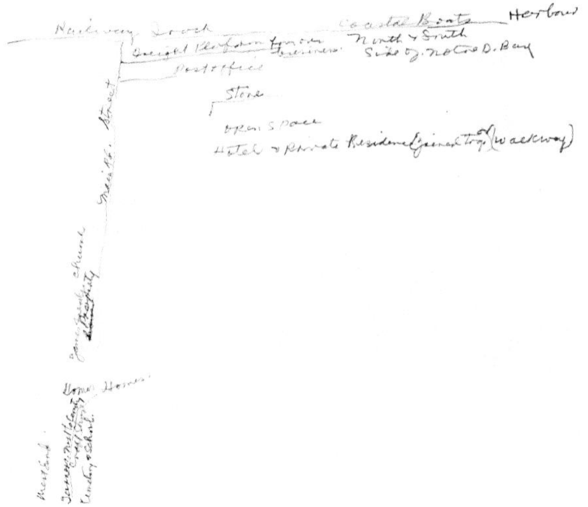

Eva Moore *née* Freake

We lived down by the railroad station. My dad, his home was up there by the church. My young days was down by the railroad station. The church was built on my grandfather's land, James Freake. Now whether I was born in their house and lived there, I don't know. All I remember is down by the railroad station. I was nineteen when I left Lewisporte. After my dad died I stayed in Lewisporte for a year. We sold our business and came into St. John's in 1929. Right here was where they used to unload our stuff for our store. Freight platform. Then you'd come up here and there was an open space, grass. Then the hotel and our private residence. It was joined with a walkway.

You'd come on up the road and you'd be up in the west end then, where Aunt Tamar Turner lived, and the cemetery and the school. I remember going to school and we'd hop down to Auntie Rowe's for a few ginger snaps, she always had ginger snaps. She said, "Put your hand down in the tin and take what you want."

The school used to be there where the craft shop is now. It's not the same building, it doesn't look like it, but it's on the very same spot. Lewisporte, I hate it the way it is now. When I think about it, I don't think it would be right for it to be the way it was. It was beautiful, quiet, serene. The housing development, it's beautiful in a sense. It wouldn't be right for me to say that I'd like Lewisporte to be like it was when I left. It was nice when I was growing up, the harbour, the boats, the skating on the harbour. We skated to school on the harbour, lots of times we did that. Then the afternoon, after you got out of school, you'd lay your books down and you'd skate and skate and skate. Then you'd pick up your books and skate home. We'd just come out from our house, go down the back lane, get out on the harbour, then you're skating all over the place, in the direction of the school. Nighttime we used to have a grand time, with a nice moon and everything. I still, when I do go out to Lewisporte, say I'm coming in by car, when I see the harbour, I get such a delight, such a thrill. My memories are really beautiful. That's it, I'm telling you. Well, my dear, it's wonderful to be a Newfoundlander.

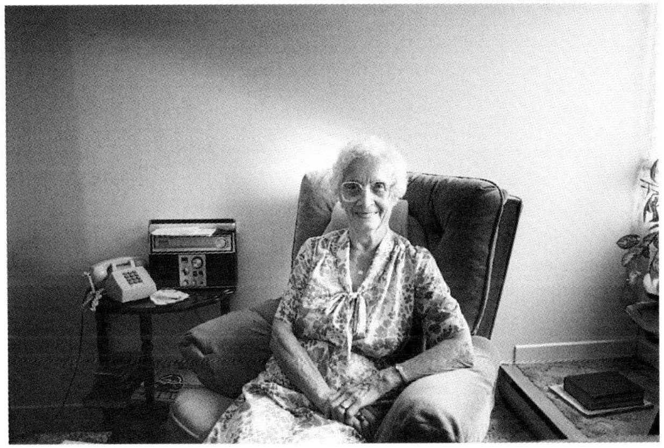

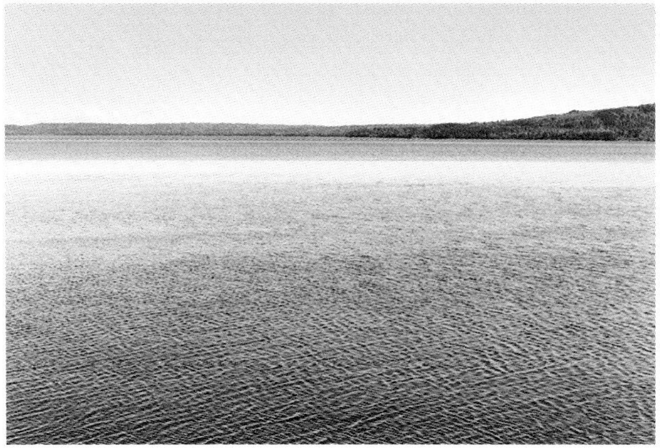

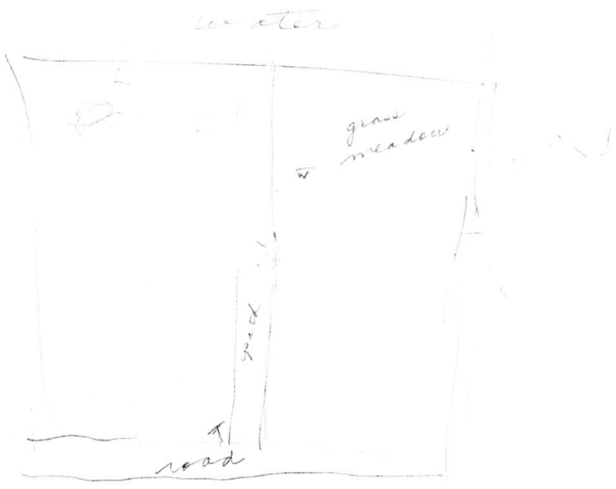

Joan Freake *née* Jewer

The house was back here. This is the cemetery side. This was the grass meadow, they used to call it. The house that's there now is right in the middle of the land, whereas Grandfather's house was over here. And the well was over here. And this is the road that went out to the gate. And this was Grandma's front garden. Over here, you went down over a slight bank and that was the water. That was fenced. The outhouse was down there. Then there was the woodhouse. This was a great big swinging gate. And this was the path. The oxen would pull the cart to come in on his own land. The woodhouse, next to the house. And this was the, well, the barn they called it, the horse's thing. This was the boundary between Grandma's land and Uncle Uriah's land. The grass meadow went from the road to the water. Because the house was back here in the corner, right near the boundary, this was why it looked like a gigantic piece of land. A child's conception. I was only nine when I lived up there. I don't know why I picture everything as being square. Now in by the house, right there, there was a damson tree and an apple tree.

I lived in Grandpa's house when I was nine, for fourteen months. Mom and I went down there to look after Grandpa and Uncle Ralph. You see, the land was Grandma Turner's land, right from the water into the track, the railroad track. It seems as if he gave more to Grandma. She got a strip from the water, crossing the road, to the track. Uncle Uriah, he went from Grandma's boundary down to the church, on the water side. And Aunt Phoebe Rowe, then, got from the road to the track. The reason that the land has passed to women is that there wasn't anyone else to give it to, only women.

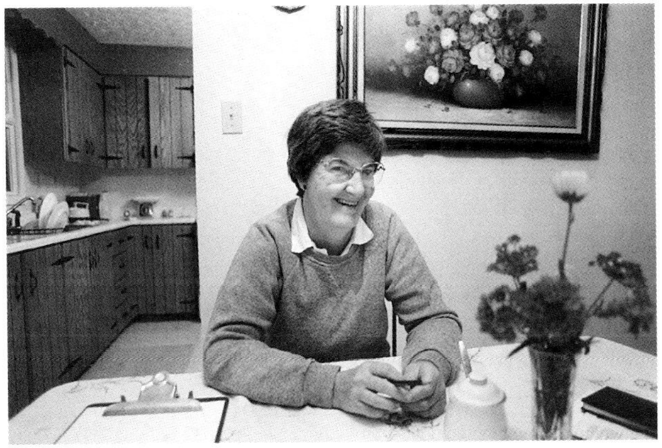

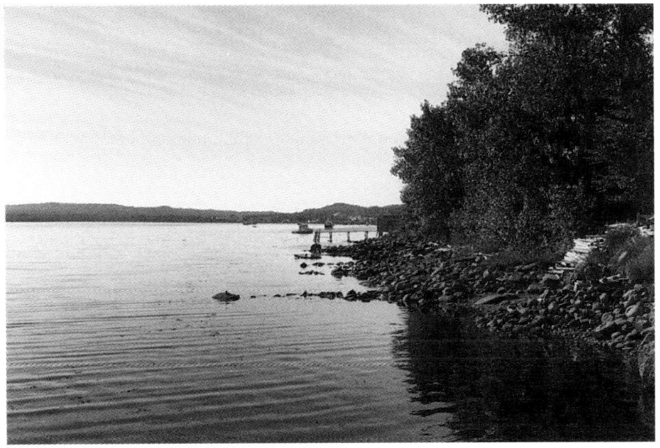

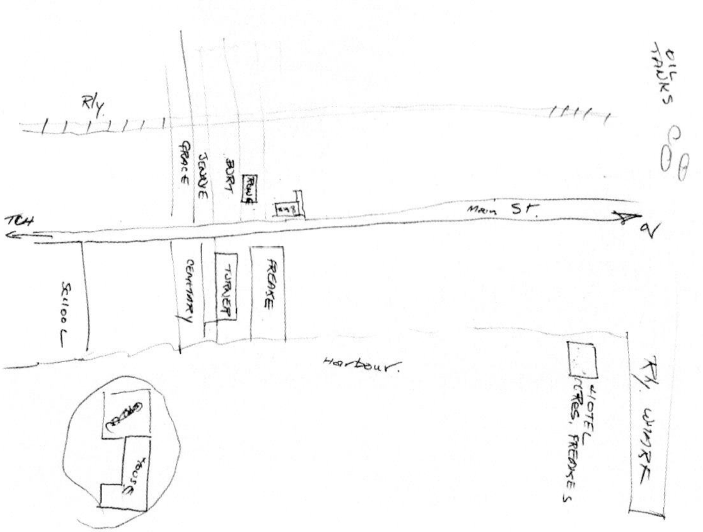

Harvey Burt

Now all this property, I'm going by hearsay from Grandmother Turner, there was a big hunk of property going right back and across the railway track and maybe even where the church is now, that was all Freake land. And that later was broken down between the Freake family into different strips. And that's the land that was my mother's, where Jennie, my sister, is now. It was given to Grandmother Turner as one of the Freakes. She in turn divided it up and my mother had a strip. Next to the strip that was given to my mother there was a strip given to her sister, Aunt Jennie, and then one to Aunt Grace.

Grandfather Turner always had a cow, oxen, a horse, pigs, geese, turkeys, sheep. He had a barn here, close to the shore. Between the house and the cemetery there was quite a large field. Part of it was garden, vegetable garden, the other part of it was grazing for the cow and the oxen. Now across the road, the property which is now where we lived, that was all a big field. And in where the house where Jennie's living in now, there was a huge barn or stable. I remember seeing all this. This was there when I was a kid.

Grandmother, she was a great one for flowers. From the front of the house right out to the road, wider than the house, was all flowers. And down toward the side of the house she had fruit trees, gooseberry bushes, raspberry, black currants, red currants, crab apples. The garden was the full width of the house. All I remember was clusters and clusters. A lot of them were high flowers. Just a mass of colour. A lot of people would come by and she'd give them a bouquet of flowers. She was a very kind woman. She used to spend half her time, besides doing all her housework, looking after sick people. I remember people coming to get her when their wife was having a baby. The doctors used to come and get her too.

I first went to school in Corner Brook because when the town was first getting built, Dad worked there in construction. But Grandmother Turner got sick. Grandfather Turner kept writing and writing, begging to have Mother to come back. She was the only one of the girls left in Newfoundland. Dad was against it. But finally he gave in, we went back to Lewisporte and we lived with Grandmother for a few years. My mother wasn't happy living there, because two families can't live together. They're bound to disagree. So Dad said, I'm going to build a house. Grandmother Turner had split the land up and Mother had this strip across the road. So this is when Dad built the house, the one Jennie's living in now. I helped to build it too, actually. And then we moved in there. We were still living with Grandmother when Jennie was born. There's twelve years difference between Jennie and I.

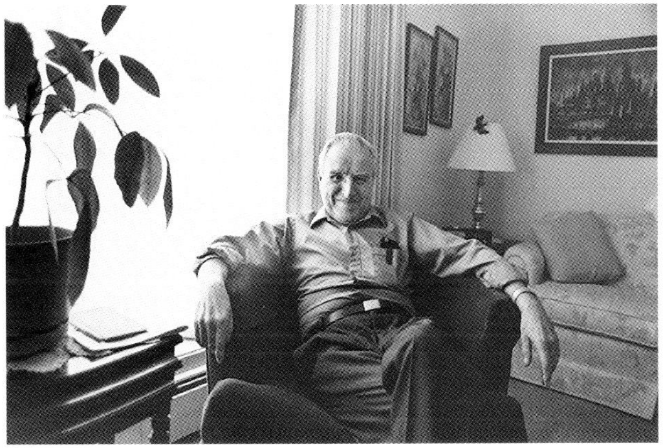

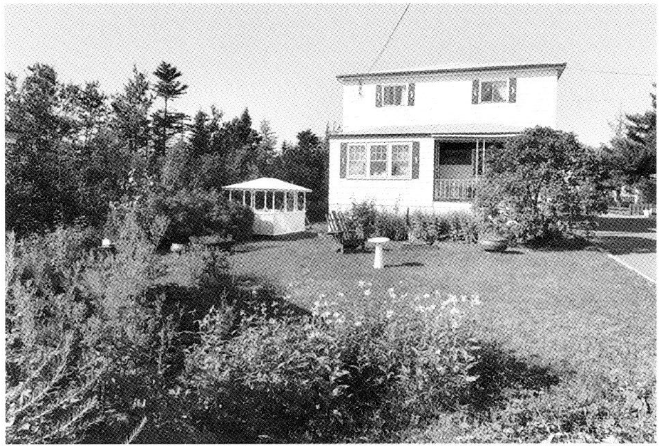

Jennie Hackett *née* Burt

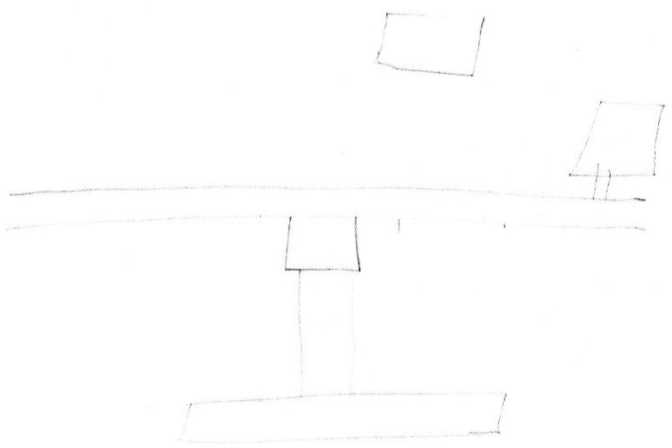

Auntie Rowe and Grandmother Turner were sisters. That land where the church is, I heard Mother say so many times that Grandmother Turner and Auntie Rowe, women now then, helped to clear that land where the church is. The house was sort of down here then. The house wasn't in the centre of the land because there was a big field and Grandfather had a bit of garden, potatoes and that, I suppose. That's the old house. It was beautiful. It had seven bedrooms, and a big attic. It should never have been torn down. It would be a landmark. The Hotel, this is what they used to call it, Turners' Hotel, because they used to have so many people staying. Grandfather was well known around because he was a camp inspector and a ship's pilot. And then he had the post office in one part of the house, in the back or something. I was born in there, in the old house. We moved in here when I was about six or seven.

This is the front garden gate to go out to the main road, only a narrow dirt road. You go out the gate, you walk down only a few steps, and you go in Auntie Rowe's house. Here's the old barn in here, a little bit to the side, where this house is to now. Grandfather had sheep and rams for breeding. And he used to keep geese. I suppose that's why there's so many stinging nettles around the place now.

Grandmother had a little flower garden out in front. This is the walk from the house out to the gate. There was a long platform out in front of the house to walk on. Flowers all around there. Now there are still some flowers there, called Mellow Sweet. Tall, like a round bed of them. Belonged to Grandmother. I see them there, nobody caring for them. And the trees down near the beach, they were on the end of the house. Aspen trees. That's one thing that hurt me so much, that the land was sold and went out of the family. And I said, I just hope he doesn't cut down those trees. I felt I just couldn't live if he cut down those big trees.

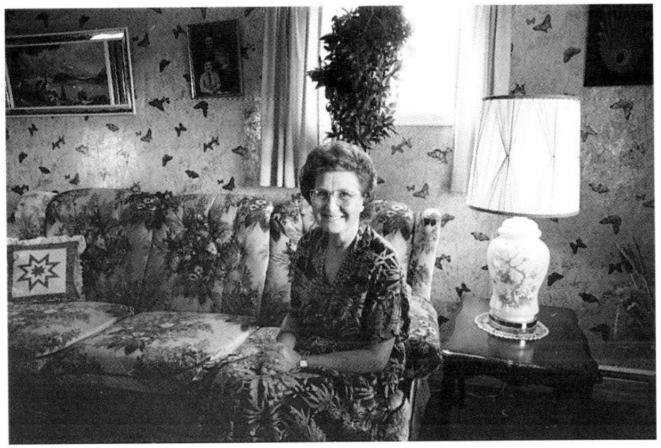
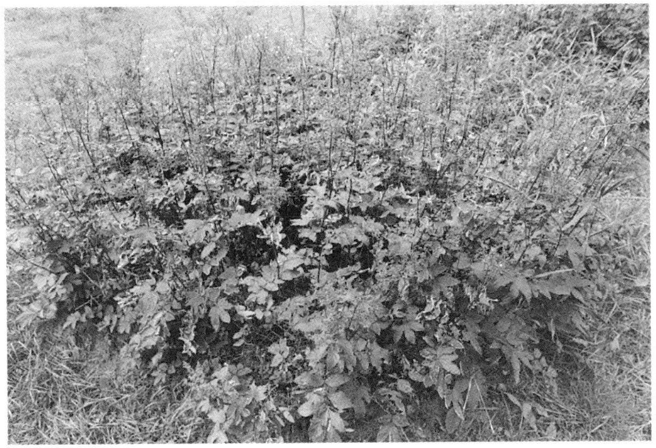
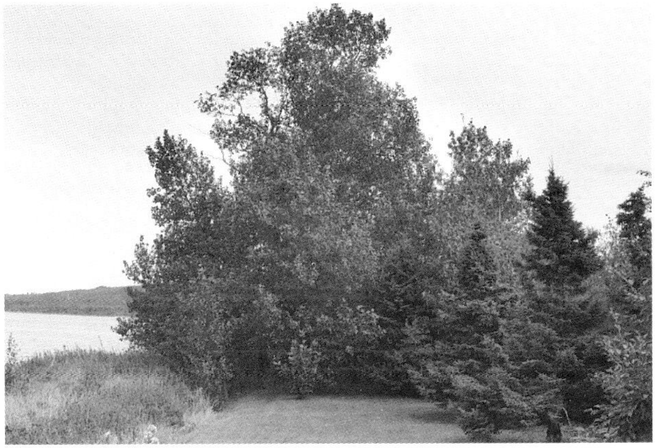
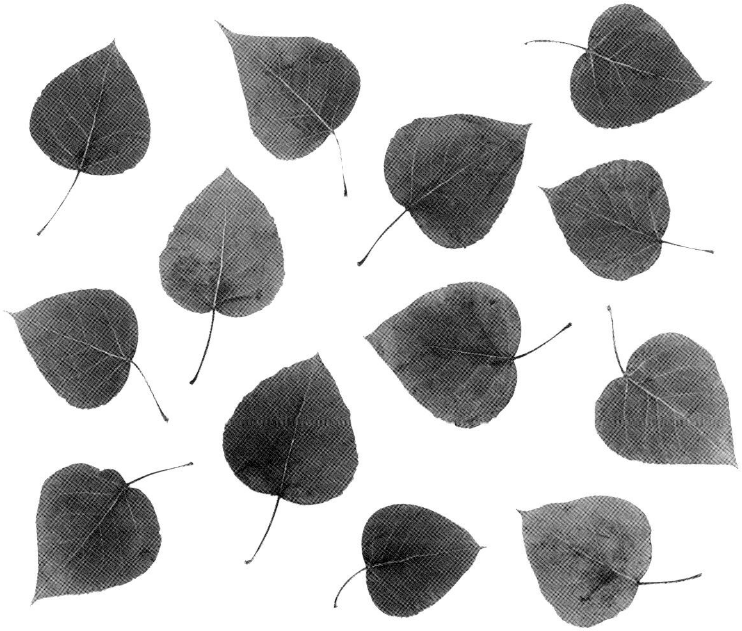

where my grandfather was born
from the series ***Places of Presence: Newfoundland kin and ancestral land, Newfoundland 1989-1991***

assemblage of:
13 black & white photographs, selenium-toned silver prints, each 8 x 10 in. (20 x 25 cm) framed,
6 memory map drawings, pencil on paper, each 8.5 x 11 in. (22 x 28 cm), framed 11 x 14 in. (28 x 36 cm),
6 story panels and 1 title panel, screen print on plexi, each 11 x 14 in. (28 x 36 cm) framed,
kelp, framed 16 x 20 in. (41 x 51 cm),
beach stone,
wooden shelf, 20 feet long x 7.25 in. deep (6 m x 18 cm).

installed dimensions: 63.5 in. high x 21.5 feet long x 7.25 in. deep (161 cm high x 6.5 m long x 18 cm deep), plus floor space.

where my grandfather was born

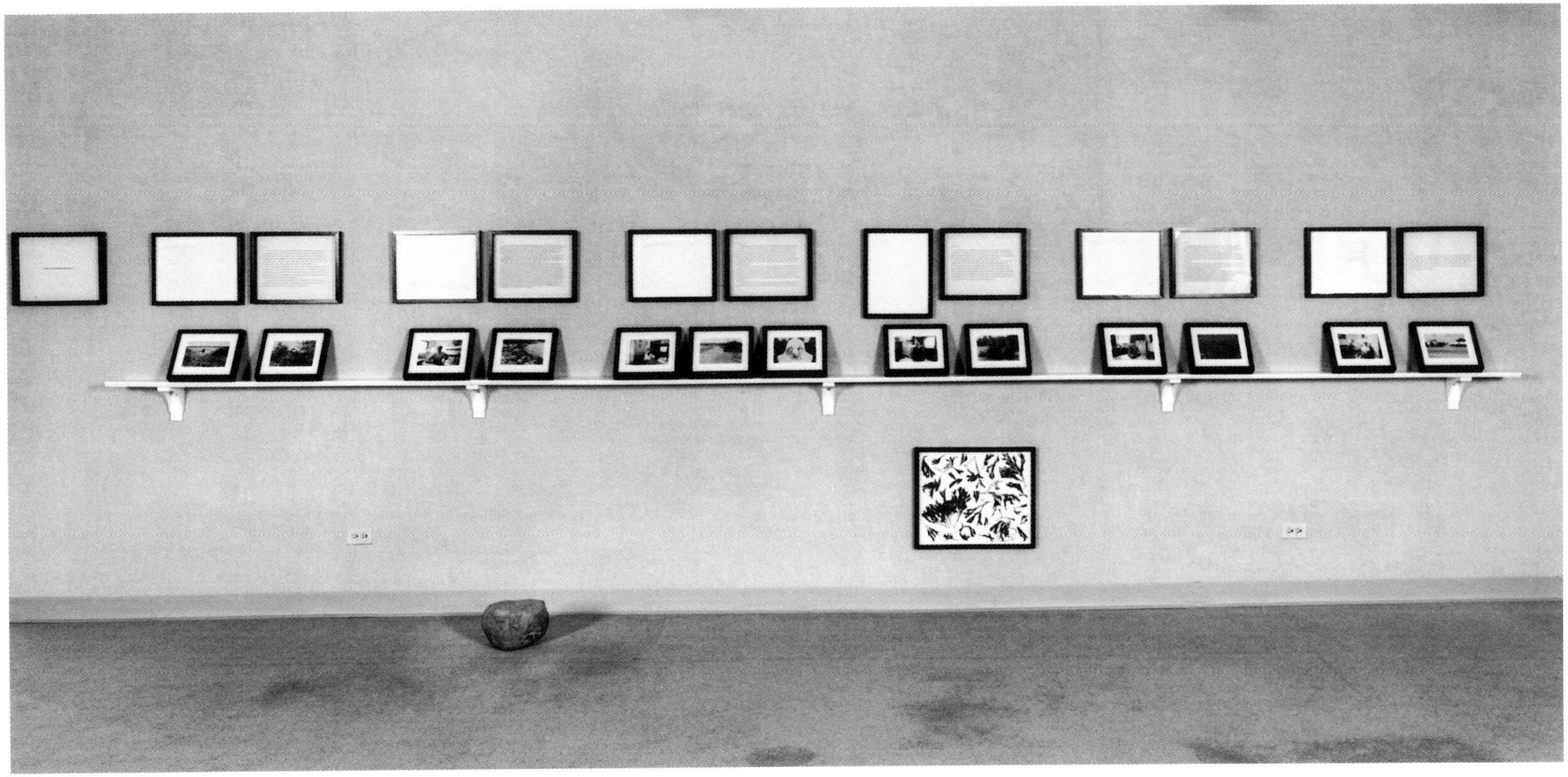

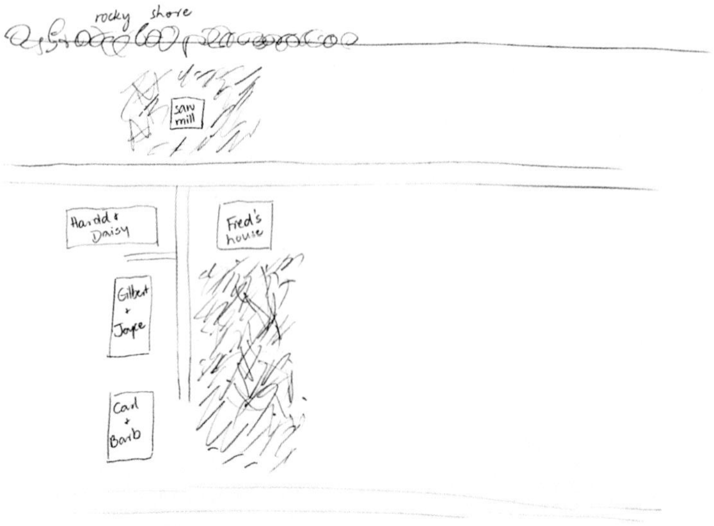

My memories

In 1981, on my first visit to Newfoundland, Mom and I went over and visited all the Laytes living on the Layte land. That would be where my grandfather was born. Now over on the Layte part of things, the land has been passed to the sons. At that time, in 1981, the old house that Gilbert Layte had been born in was still standing. And they were talking about tearing it down because they all, the four brothers who are still living on the land, each has his own house and nobody was looking after the old home. Anyway the house is gone now, this is ten years later, 1991, and there's an empty grassy spot where that house used to be.

The other thing I remember and appreciate is that the shoreline is still all rocky and wild. The reason that the land on the water side is kind of wild is because Fred still keeps the old saw from when they ran a sawmill there. He keeps it in a little shed and he keeps the shed painted. The property all around is grown up with bushes and long grass, and the shore is rocky. I've collected a beach rock from there and I've spent a lot of time just being there, on the shore, thinking about the people who walked there before me.

The other part that I love on the Layte property is in back of Fred's house. He's got lots of old currant bushes and a big old apple tree, and he's got his woodpile. Around the other brothers' houses they've put in tidy grassy lawns.

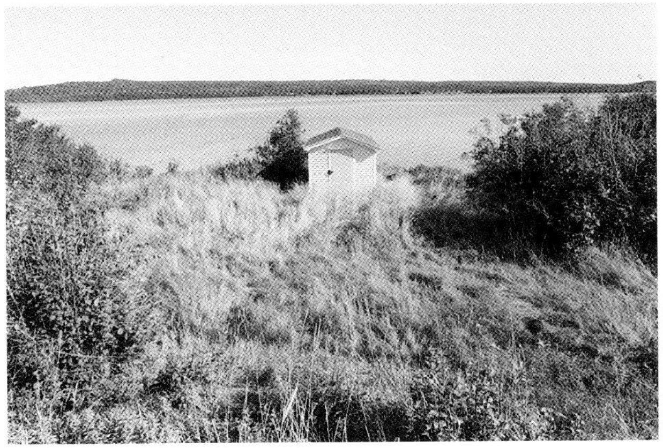

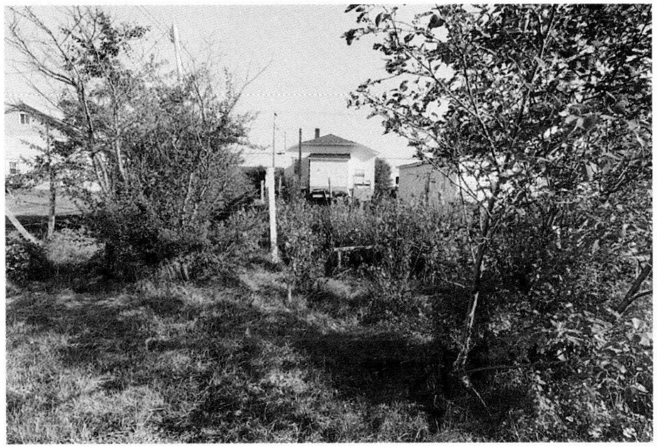

Fred Layte

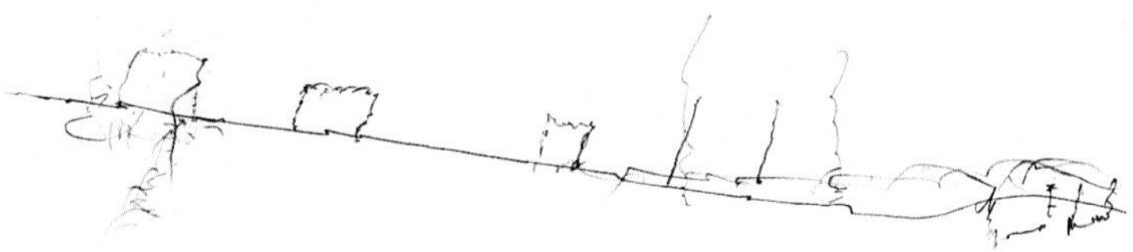

I was born in 1908. Father was born here and he was ninety-two when he died. They was all healthy people then. You know, then, if they cut their finger, they'd pick elderblossom and they'd make a bread poultice. Well, they'd soak the bread, see, and make a poultice, sprinkle the elderblossom on it and that would cure the cut. There was a big tree in there, that's where my grandmother, your great-grandmother, used to get her elderblossom. Oh what a beautiful tree. He was right white, just as if he was painted. She used to pick her elderblossom and put them out in the sun on a sheet. Could be a flour bag or a blanket.

This would be the land down here, James Layte's land, my grandfather. The road is in here. Now this road is what everybody in Lewisporte gave the government. Twelve feet of road. They used to have to go down around the beach to go to church. Walk over the beach rocks, right down around the shore. Every man joined together and gave them twelve feet. That's what James Layte done. They made the road right through Lewisporte. We only had a road for a horse and cart then. No cars here then.

James Layte married in Fogo. Elizabeth came somewhere from Fogo Island. He was fishing over there, then he shift in here, Lewisporte. Nobody here in Lewisporte. Well, not many. They took up this piece of land here. He just come in and settled it. 'Twas granted in his name. A square block of land. It goes in there about half a mile. His boys got it. This is Arthur's block, then Alfred's, then Uncle John, and then George, your mother's father, and then next to that was Albert. I think that's how she's lined up now. Every man wanted a piece of land right to the seashore. Your grandfather had it to the beach. Every man had his piece of land, his strip. They haven't got it now, see. Got it sold. This is the only part with Laytes now. Only for me, they'd have it all gone. I fought. Not going to sell it, not going to sell it, no sir. The old skipper too, my father, he didn't want to sell it. This is the Laytes, right here. I think 'twas all right. They're still at it, still want to sell it, inside the track and out there against the water. I'm not selling my share. I've got this place here and I loves it. I'm free on me own place. Born here, in there on that spot that Carl is on. It seems good to me for a bunch of Laytes to be in the one place. Now, sometime perhaps they'll want to get to the water. I can't go on another man's land if they sell it. I've got to go on my own part, if I've got it. I can have a wharf there if I want it. All the rest sold theirs to different people. There's different people living on it now. I'd have been in favour of keeping the Laytes on it. Your grandfather, he might have wanted a bit of money.

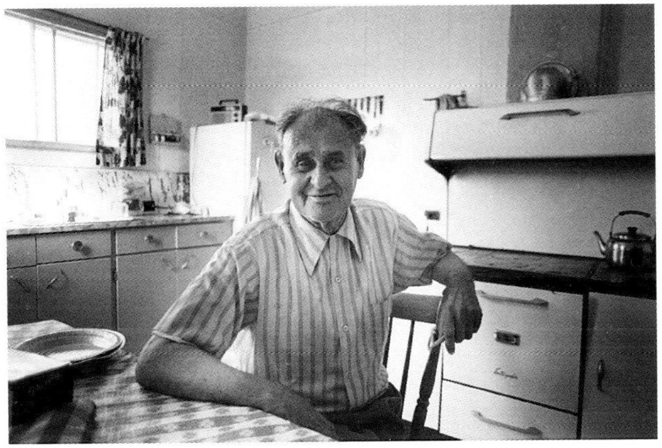

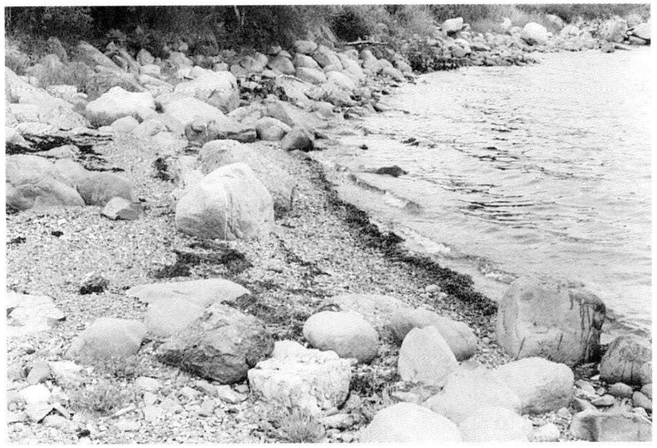

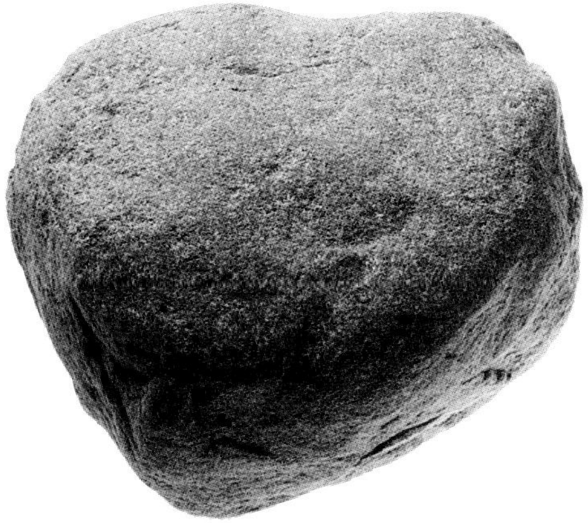

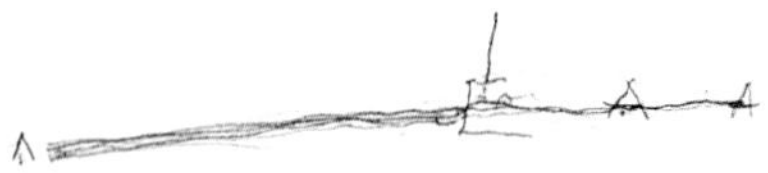

Effie Kavli *née* Layte

Old Grandmother Layte, she used to live with my mother. My dear, what a job we used to have to keep her, she used to run away from us. She'd go down the big long lane from our house, right back where Carl has his house now. The poor old soul. She'd look back to see if we were watching her, and when she'd get out to the road, my dear, go. She could go like the wind. Just as quick as that. That's true what I'm telling you. She used to say she was going up to Aunt Mary Layte's, Aunt Mary and Uncle John's. As far as I'm concerned, she wanted to get away, to get free. She was old, but she was smart. She dressed in a nice black dress and black shoes. And a full skirt, right down to her ankles. Sometimes a white lace collar. Sometimes I gets her in my eyes now.

There was our house there, see. That's the only house that was there then, in that long lane. There was nobody else. Say this is our long lane, going out. There was the road then. The beach was out here. She used to turn and go on up that way. There she is there now, going on up that way. Then was Uncle John's next to ours, right on the corner of the road. And then Albert's. It seemed like the Laytes was all in a line, you know. Alfred was up the road, he lived right here. George went away to Toronto and he never came back. That's what happened to him.

In the night you know, they didn't used to have the lights. Dark black nights. But the thing I used to hate was to pass the graveyard. The white headstones, that used to bother me. I'd turn and look the wrong way.

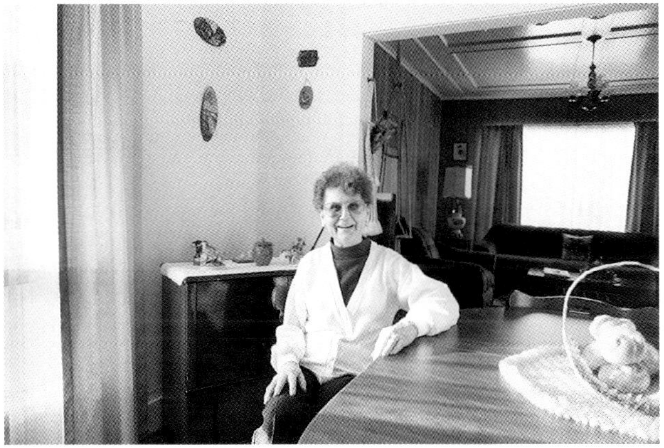
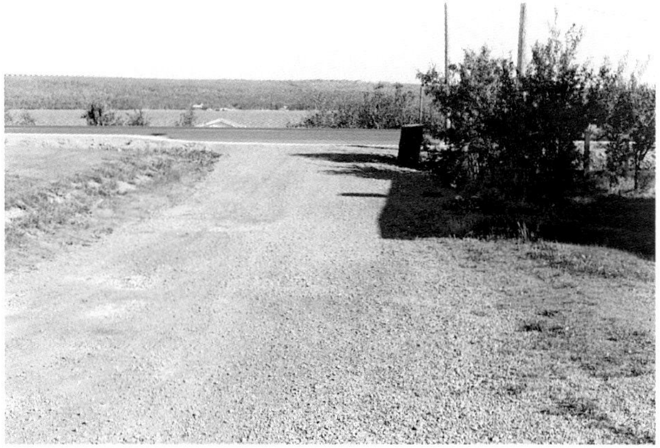
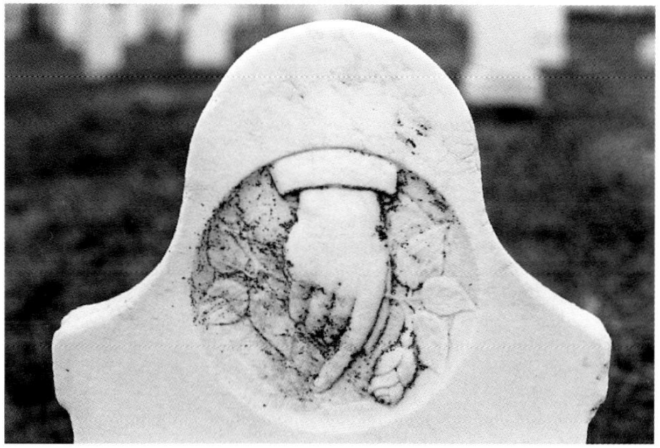

Harold Layte

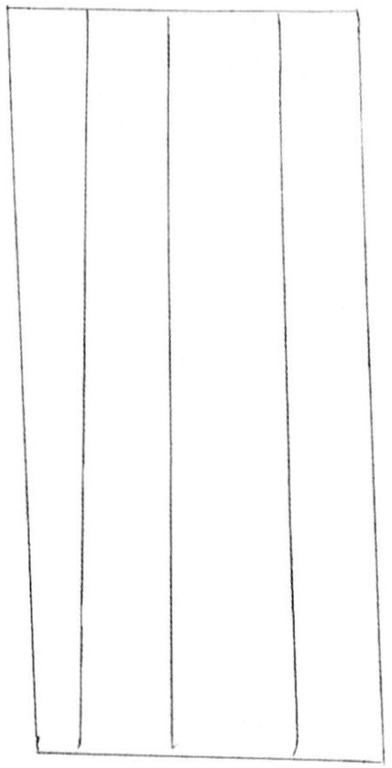

You don't want me to put it the way it is now. No. The way it was then. Now my markings are not fair. The land runs from the salt water into the country. Looking to the left, this is Albert's, and John's, and Alfred's, and Arthur's. George, see, he was gone. All I know is the four brothers were living here. I don't know if George was in between here and gave over the land to one of his brothers or not when he left.

My father had a sawmill down by the water. We had a wharf, a little pier, for a dory. Years ago, you know, they'd get kelp for the gardens. They'd go across the harbour and get a boatload and bring it across. I remember that. Fred and Father, you know. Father had a big garden there where Gilbert got his house now. Potatoes, turnip, cabbage, and carrots. That's what you'd live on, one time. Oh we had wonderful gardens. Father had a cellar. It was a wooden frame inside. And it was all buried over with earth and then it was sodded all over. Little bins inside for the vegetables. I can almost see it now, it was out from Father's house. You see where the alders are there, it was right there. They'd have a door, a double door, where the frost wouldn't get in. You go in there, in the winter, and oh my, some warm. Underground, see.

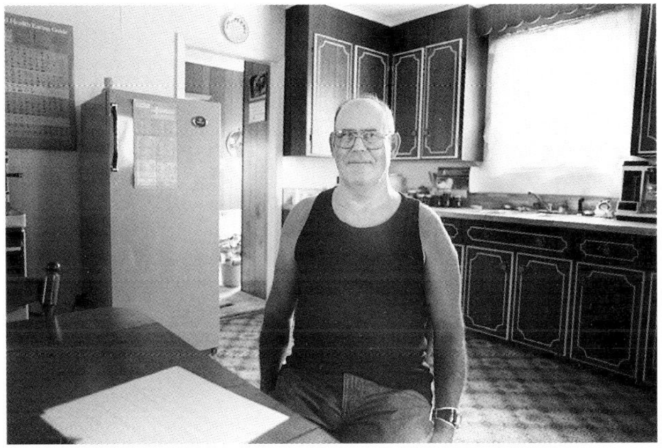

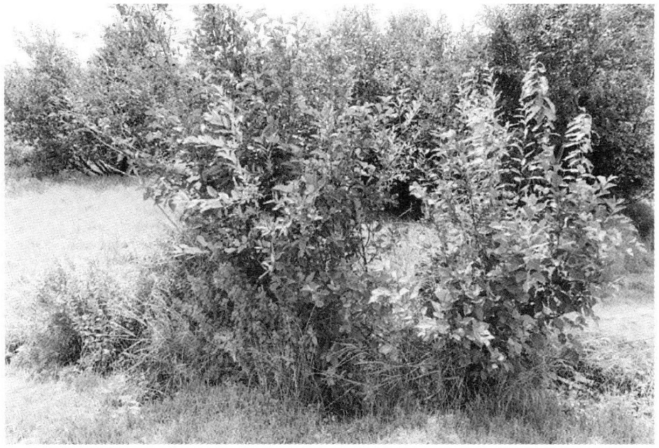

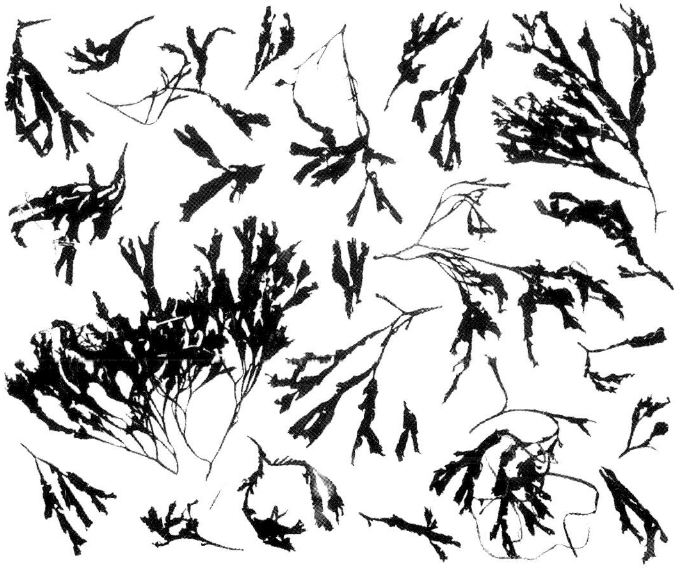

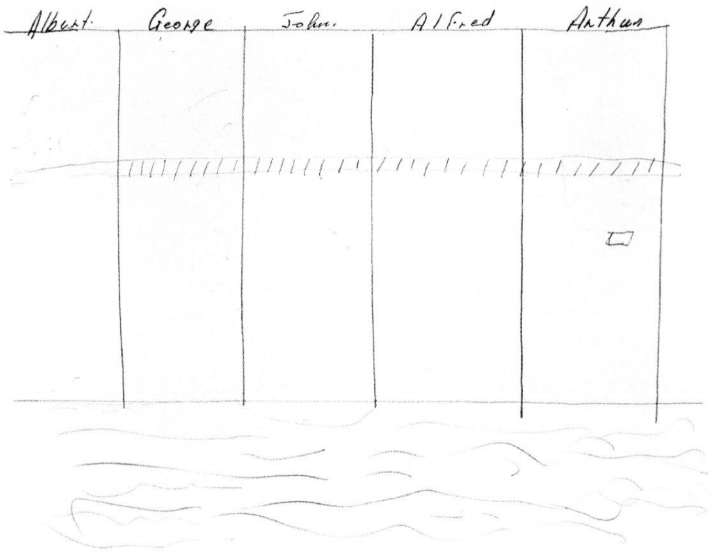

Gilbert Layte

I believe it was something like this. As far as I'm concerned, this is how it was. It's not a straight line. It's on an angle. The water's here. I believe it's wider outside than it is inside. Well, my love, that's as far as I know how it goes. You saw the old house, didn't you, the house I was born in. We had to take it down. Burned it. Used it for kindling. If Mom knew what I'd done to her house she'd kill me. Yes, she'd flatten me.

Let's take the railroad track across here. Roughly out there. And that's where the house was. Father built it himself. Money was some scarce. The house was right up on that little hill, this side of Carl's. Deteriorated you know. I believe it was built in 1914. We tore it down about five years ago, 1983, 1984. So that'll give it seventy years. Could be that. That's where it was to. And out behind the house there was a well and that was where we got all our water.

Dark, nighttime, you wouldn't see anything. Only if someone came with a white cap, and then you wouldn't know what it was until they were alongside of you. The kitchen would be on the inside side. You'd have your oil lamp on the table and you'd do whatever work you had to do. There'd be no light then on the front until you went to bed. You wouldn't see a bit of light. Now it's only flick on your light.

This was all woods. And where that road is to, that was woods. Big alders, trees and one thing and another. All this here where I'm to, was all trees. James Layte, your great-grandfather, was the first one that settled on this land. He come in here, see, and he settled. By and by he got it measured and he got a grant for it. They went to work and cleared it all out. Grandmother had a garden. There wasn't too many here when he settled in Lewisporte. He must have been pretty handy the first that settled here. They don't spell their name in Fogo like we spell ours. I imagine 'tis all the same Laytes. There's no one bothered about a record at that time.

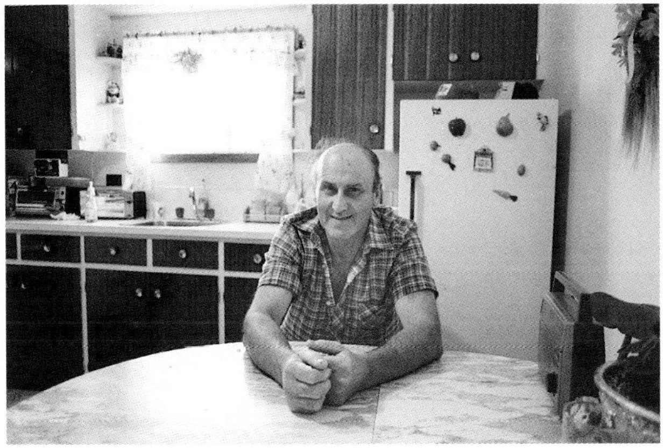

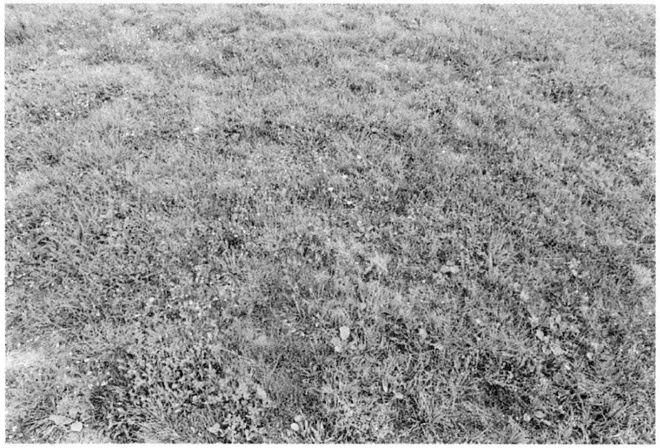

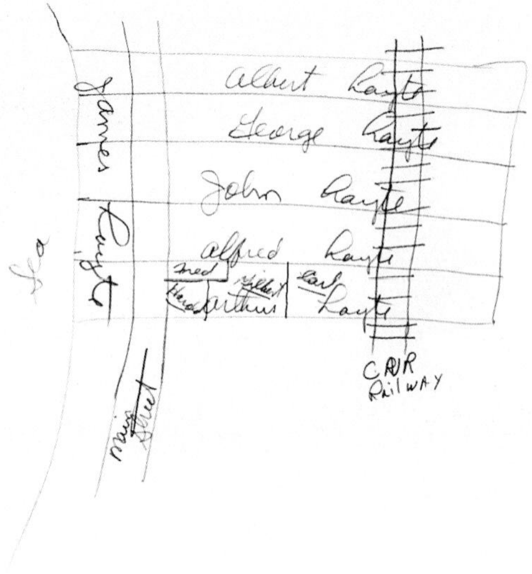

Carl Layte

Now this is going to be a rough diagram, Marlene, very rough. This is not drawn to scale. This is freehand. Arthur's, then Alfred's, then John's. Now the last two up there, George's, and the last one up was Albert's. There you go. That's the land there. That's the main street there. This way too was the railroad track. James Layte got the grant for the full block of land, 1800s or something around. He died around 1905. I'm going on memory again, I mightn't be that close. We're on Arthur's block. I'll mark in ours. There you go. Now don't look at that and say one fellow got more than the other.

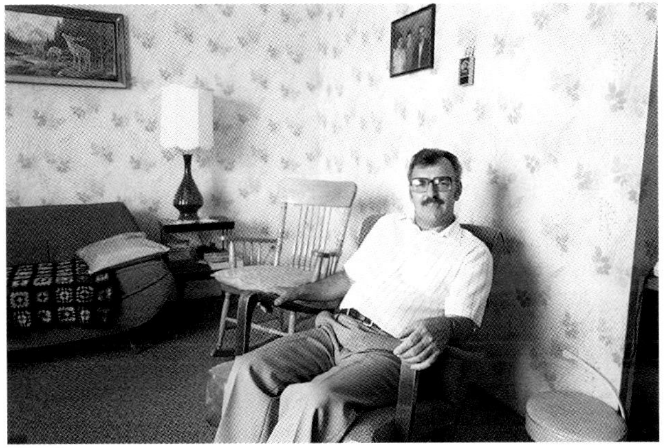

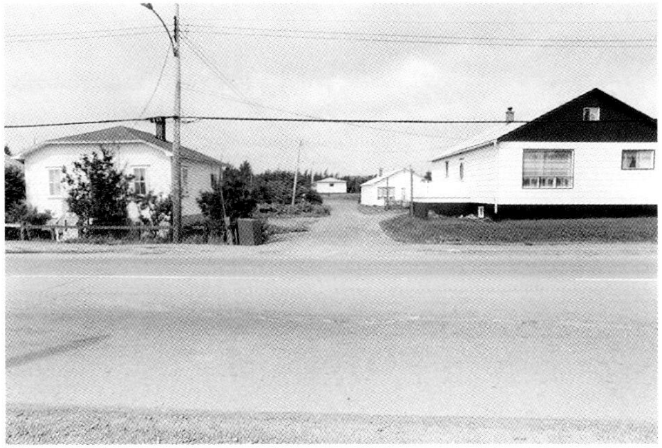

where my great-grandmother was born
from the series ***Places of Presence: Newfoundland kin and ancestral land, Newfoundland 1989-1991***

assemblage of:
14 black & white photographs, selenium-toned silver prints, each 8 x 10 in. (20 x 25 cm) framed,
6 memory map drawings, pencil on paper, each 8.5 x 11 in. (22 x 28 cm), framed 11 x 14 in. (28 x 36 cm),
7 story panels and 1 title panel, screen print on plexi, each 11 x 14 in. (28 x 36 cm) framed,
2 stones,
5 birch logs,
wooden shelf, 23 feet long x 7.25 in. deep (7 m x 18 cm).

installed dimensions: 63.5 in. high x 24.5 feet long x 7.25 in. deep (161 cm high x 7.5 m long x 18 cm deep), plus floor space.

where my great-grandmother was born

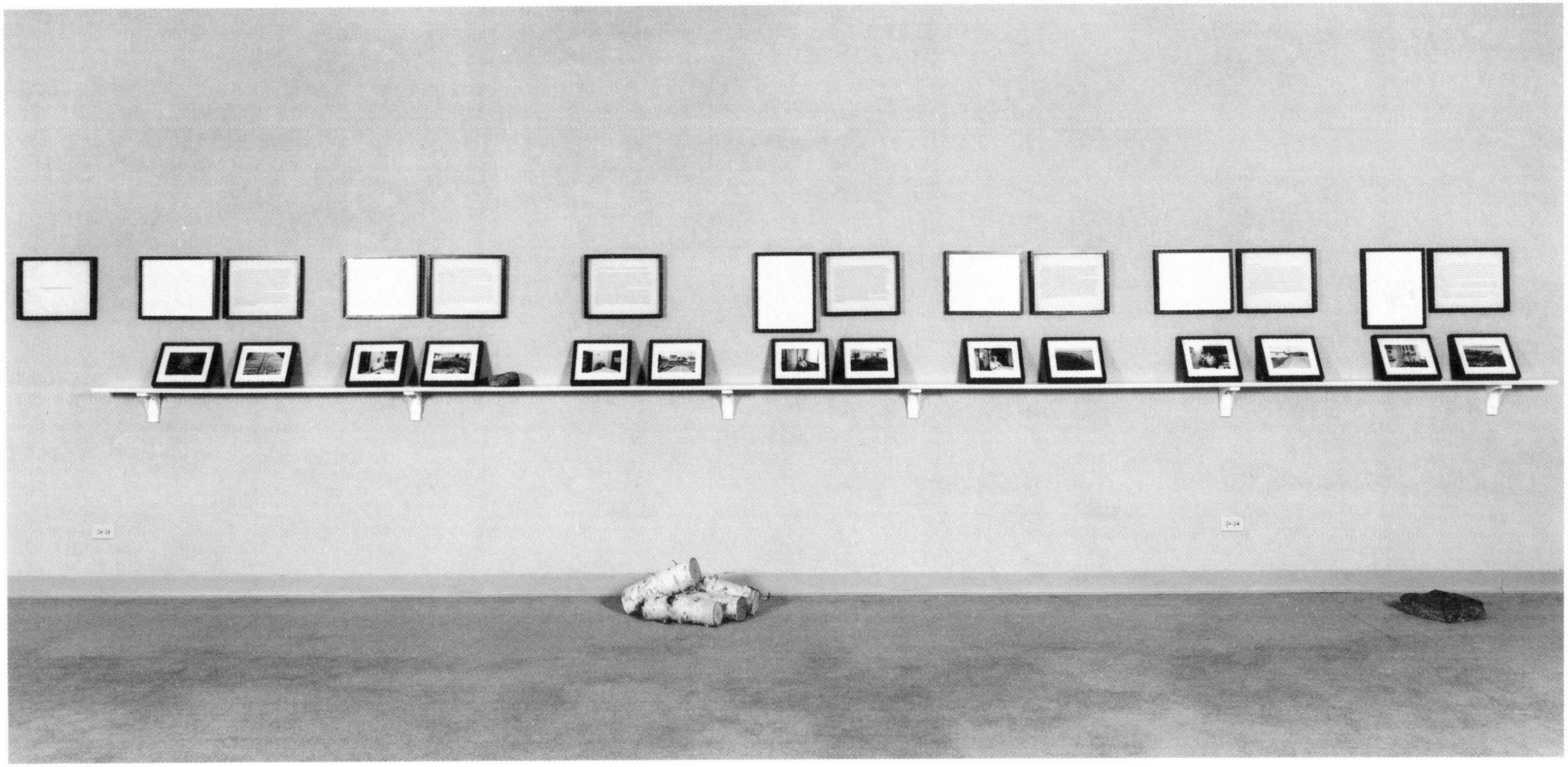

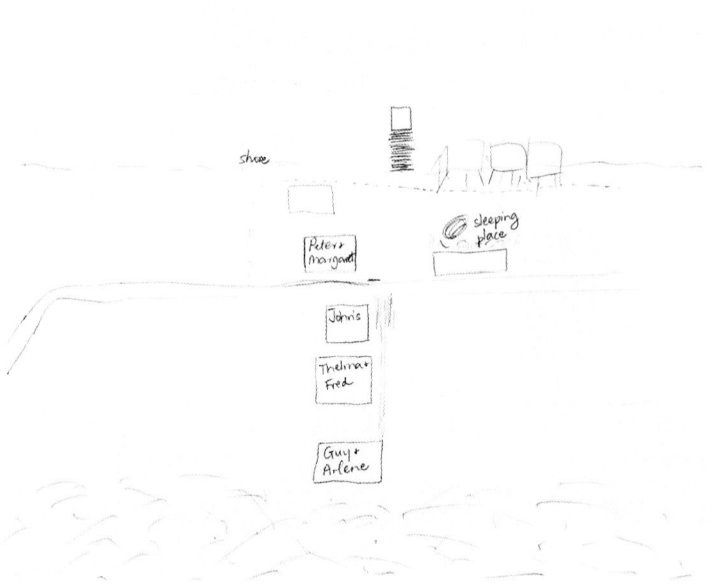

My memories

I first went to Fogo Island in 1982, when I was on a camping trip around Newfoundland. The reason I went there was because Bert Freake in Lewisporte had told me that Tamar Freake, my great-grandmother, was born there and the origins of that end of the family had been in Joe Batt's Arm. So I crossed on the ferry over to Fogo Island. That night I set up my tent in the tiny bit of yard in back of John Freake's house, right next to the flowers. That's where I slept that night and then I left the next day. Later I found out that John's brother, Fred, lived in the house right behind, and his other brother, Peter, lives in the house right across the road. Well then, I've been back to Fogo Island several times since then and I met Fred and Peter. One time when I was there, I spent a few nights sleeping on the spot where the house stood that my great-grandmother Tamar had been born in. The reason I knew that was the spot, was because Bert Freake had drawn a memory map for me. But of course that house is gone and there's just a grassy area there now. And when I was there after Fred had died, the year after Fred had died, I guess, I stayed with Thelma, Fred's wife, in her house.

I also spent a lot of time with Peter and his wife, Margaret. Thelma and Margaret took turns inviting me for meals, so I was back and forth between the two houses. Peter showed me the old fishing gear in the shed, and I especially remember the old stage made out of long sticks. It's one of the best places in Newfoundland, Joe Batt's Arm is, for seeing all the individual stages still along the shore. In most places, the fishermen have given up keeping up their stages because they use community wharves now. This stage has a beautiful pattern of silvery-grey worn sticks that you walk along.

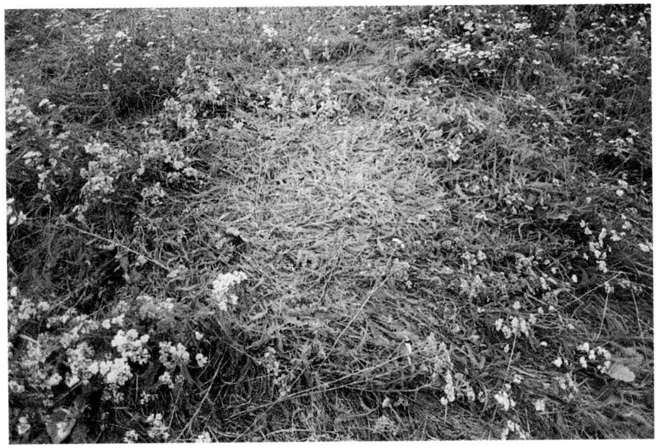

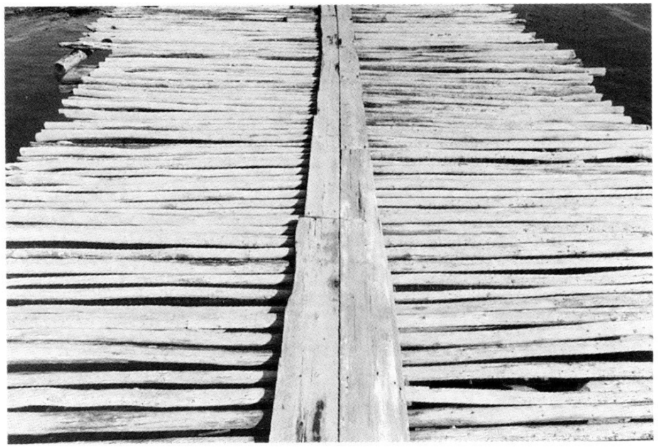

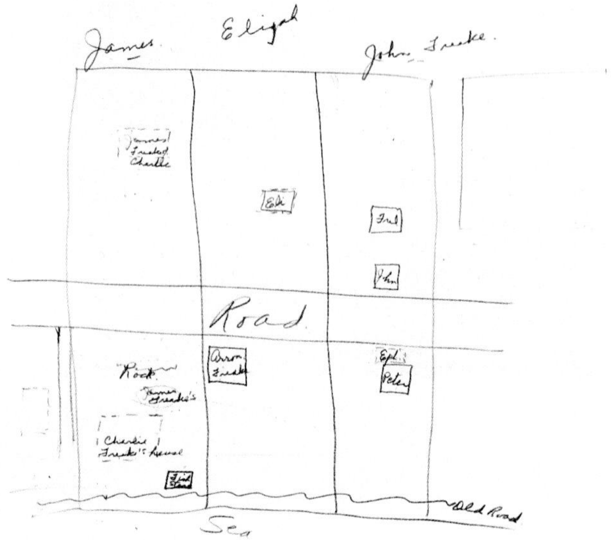

Bert Freake

Here was the section of land, it goes to the seashore. Now then, the road goes through it like this. This is John Freake's land, John, my great-grandfather. This is Elijah's here. And this is James', your great-great-grandfather. We lived over here. Now then, right here there's a huge rock. They've probably got it blasted. Your great-great-grandfather's house was right here. I'm probably the only one who knows that, I'll tell you, because Dad remembers where James Freake's house was. Are you still making your art mainly with rocks? You should get a piece of rock from where your great-great-grandfather's house was. Tamar, your great-grandmother, she was born where I'm telling you the house was.

If they sold a house, this was Freake premises. They wouldn't allow anybody to live within this section. Every house that was sold, they were all moved off the land. There's five houses that were sold that I can remember. I remember Dad saying that they couldn't sell the land, they could only sell the house. There were twelve houses in this section here. When I grew up they were occupied houses. They were filled. When Peter's father and my grandfather lived there, they just had room for their stages and flakes. You could walk from flake to flake. All the flakes were joined together. The women were responsible to see that the fish, after it was cleaned and split, was salted properly. Then it would have to be washed and dried, and the women were responsible for all that. They had to be experts, to see that it was perfectly dry. Actually, fish today, I wouldn't eat it.

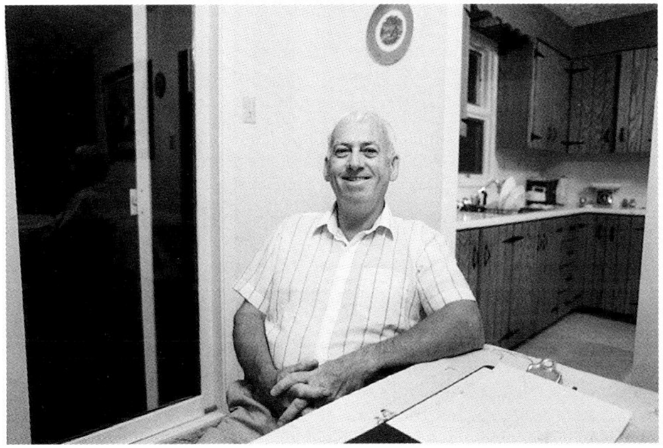
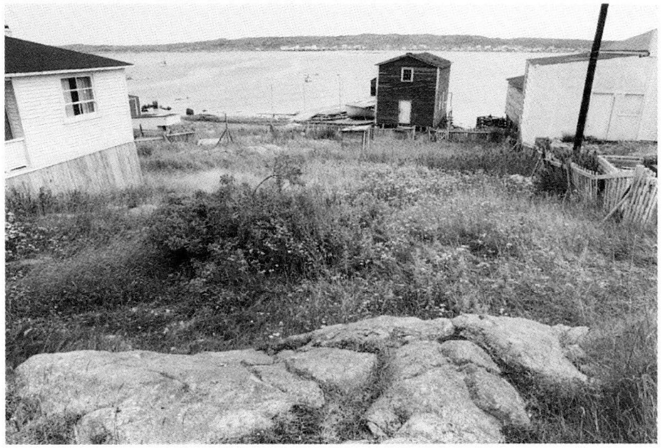
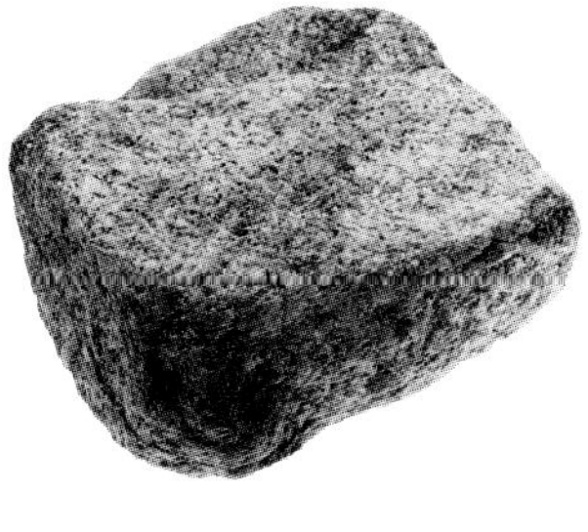

Ephraim Freake

I'm seventy-one now. Sixty years ago, all the people thought about was fish. You couldn't blame your parents for that, that's the way things were. I educated myself. I left Fogo in 1940 and I never went back there to live.

I'm the youngest of nine. On the inside of the road there was John the oldest, then Fred the next oldest. That's the two you met. John died May third this year, Fred died last year in July month. Then there's Charlie next oldest. He's been passed away about thirty-five years, I suppose. Then there's Ken's. That's the four houses on the inside of the road. There's only two houses there now, that's John's and Fred's. The outside is the water side. Inside is inside the road. Peter is on the outside of the road, that's where my father's house used to be, nearby there. You know, I haven't got a picture of that old house. Fred's youngest son, Guy, he's built up his own house in the back of the garden. It was one strip of land running in from the water, running back to the hill. On the other side there was my father's brothers, Charlie and Eli. Their land was the same, one strip of land running in from the water. There's only one living there now, Uncle Eli's son's son, Doug Freake. There were a lot of Freakes what we call down the shore and up the shore.

There were trees there, what we call on the back of Fogo, but on the outside where we lived there were no trees at all. You'd have to go in the schooners in October. We'd go up around Lewisporte and these places. You'd go in, cut it down with an axe. Then spilling it out, that's what we used to call it, carrying it out on your shoulder. About eight feet long from the woods. Bring it out to the landwash, put it aboard a small boat, what we call a punt, take it out to the schooner, throw it up and put it aboard the schooner. About fifteen hundred pieces of wood is roughly what we could take on the schooner. Then you'd go home to Joe Batt's Arm and take it ashore from the schooner. Then share it among the four houses. That would be my father's, John's, Fred's, and Charlie's. You'd saw it up in about foot long junks. That would be the heat for the winter. It would take about eight to ten days. Oh my, only the fittest survived, my dear. I don't know if it's better or for worse, everything is so modernized.

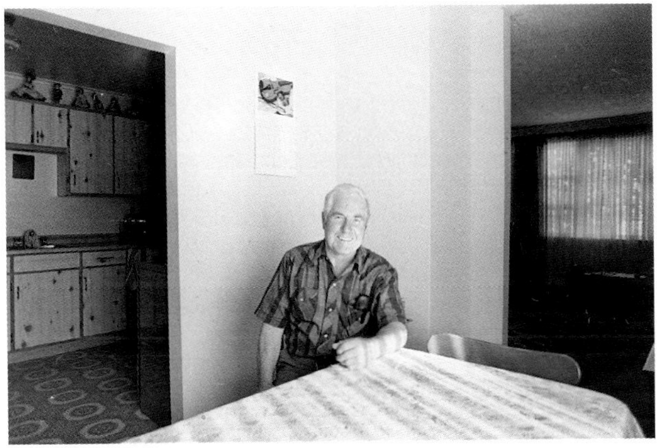

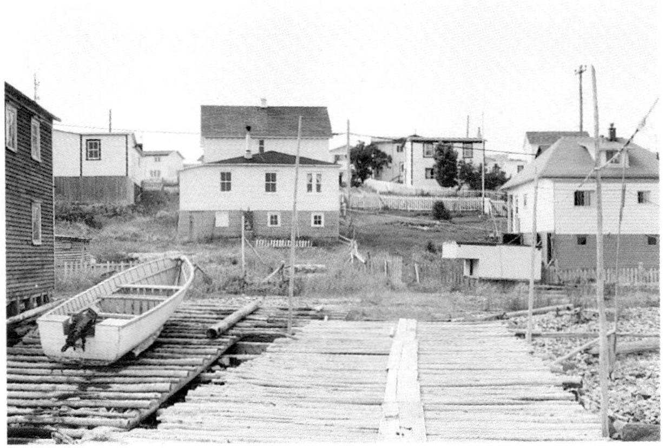

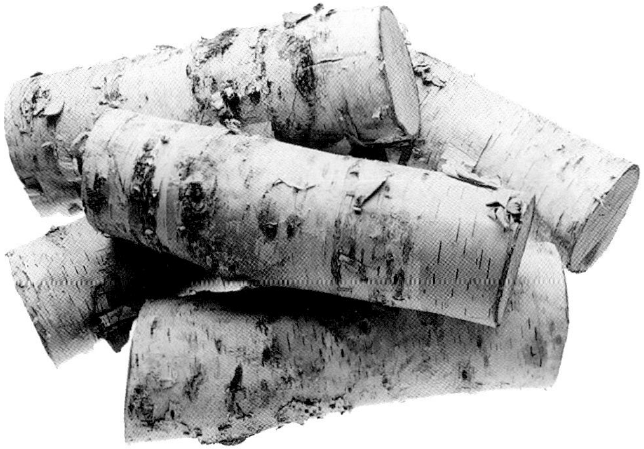

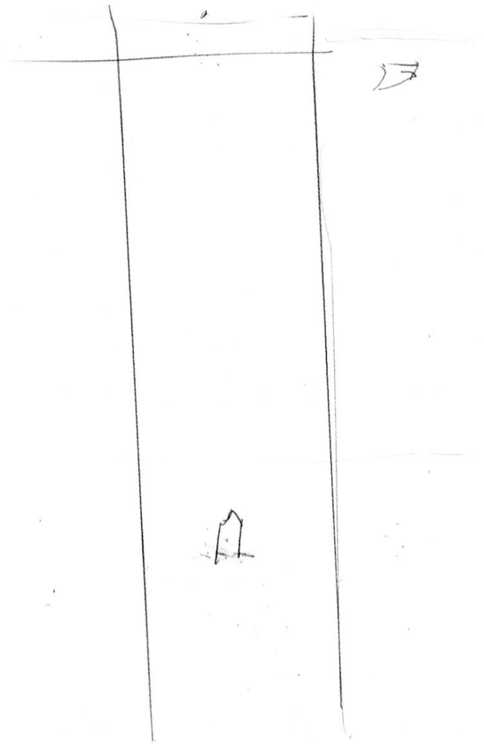

Peter Freake

The land runs down here and this is the water there. John Freake's, this would be here, Grandfather's. Aaron, my cousin, said, "I can remember that old house, it was right there," and he said that you had to go out-of-doors and go up steps and go back in to go to bed. Say Elijah was next. And James. James gave his land to Uncle Charlie. None of their offspring, the two brothers who went to Lewisporte, lives here in Joe Batt's Arm, only of Grandfather John's. On this block now, my father's house was here. My house next to it. Now across the road was John's and Fred's and Charlie's, my brothers. And Kenneth's. My house is only about three feet from the end of Grandfather's strip. And there, close to Aaron's, is where it ends. So they're not very wide, about fifty-five feet. Where Doug's shop is, is where John's house was, John of Charlie. That house was moved over there, in that garden there. It burned about three years ago. James, that's Bert's father, that house was just up one side of that white bungalow there. Before John's house was moved there, Herbert's house was there. And that was sold and then moved. Kenneth's house was there, where Guy's is. That's moved up the shore a little way, just up here. Charlie's house was moved. Ken's house was moved. Herbert's house was moved. John's. James'. That's five. And Uncle Eli's. That's six houses that were moved off this land. And Uncle Charlie's, that's Bert's grandfather, it went across the harbour in wintertime, across the ice. It was pulled there by manpower. You know, we often talk about the little space here now for the houses. But you wouldn't believe how many houses were here at one time. They were all in line with one another, all crammed in with one another. My father's house was there, right about where that little tree is now. I believe it was moved three different times. You'd think it would fall to pieces, but no way, it was built that strong. Oh, you'd get a whole lot of people to help out. You'd go and knock on the doors a couple of days before, and say when you're going to be ready. There would be four hundred men, two hundred men, all according to the size of the house. Big long rope. That would be something to see now, wouldn't it, a crowd of men pulling a house.

We were all fishermen. So father and us had our fishing stage here, Uncle Eli here, and Uncle Charlie there. There was all stages all along by the shore one time. Years ago there was all schooners tied up along here. There's one stage left, Uncle Eli's. But Guy owns it now. One hundred years old, it could be up so far as that. Uncle Eli built that.

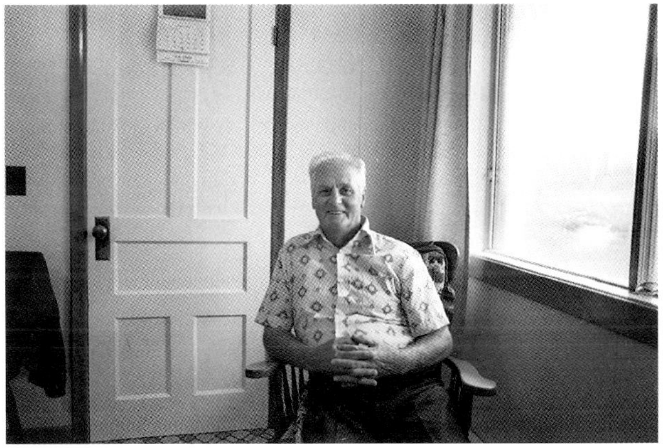
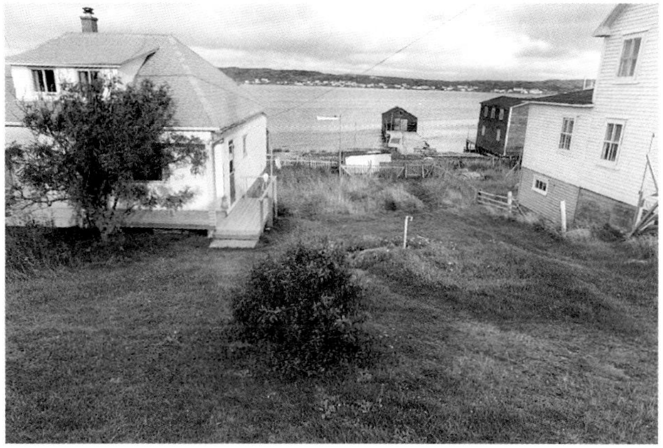

Nellie Decker *née* Freake

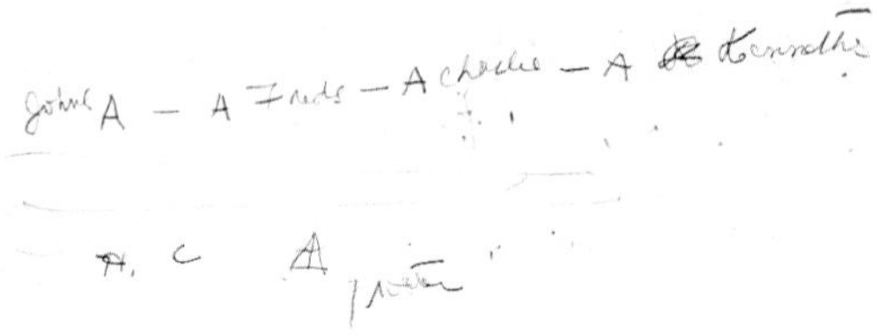

Dad's house was the house down here, below the road. John's. Fred's. Charlie's. Kenneth's. They followed up the garden like that, one after the other. They built their houses as close to the seashore as they could get it because of fishing. When the boys married and wanted land to build their houses on, each one of the brothers had their strip of land. John built his house first, then Fred's. That was a big garden, all grass. My father had a horse. Our horse was small, really small. Little Jim. And Uncle Charlie had Big Jim, and he was big too. Mom had goats. I grew potatoes and cabbage. And I had a teacher, and when I brought cabbage down for her to cook, she'd say, "Look, the day I'd grow cabbage like that I'd give up teaching."

Dad had land up on the bottom of Joe Batt's Arm. And each one of the sons had a patch. We'd row up the harbour, in a punt, and carry up cods' heads. We'd put them in a barrel and row and take them up in buckets to fertilize the cabbage. If you tell some of the things you did fifty years back, they'd say you were boasting. You just did what you had to do. You go out there now and there's not a flake. Every flake, every stage is gone. Nothing. Look, if we didn't have our memories we wouldn't have much, would we. Listen, there's not so much there to miss now. You go up on Freakes' room, Fred is gone, John is gone. Nothing left there now. Memories is all.

It's not the same anymore. In them days, as soon as you were big enough to help, even if you couldn't make a faggot, lay down so many fish, you could yaffle it, pick up an armful at one time. Put your two arms underneath it. Spread it all out on boughs, head and tail, head and tail. You could fit more together doing it that way. If you were nine years old there was something you could do to help. Even if you just picked up a few and carried them along by the tail.

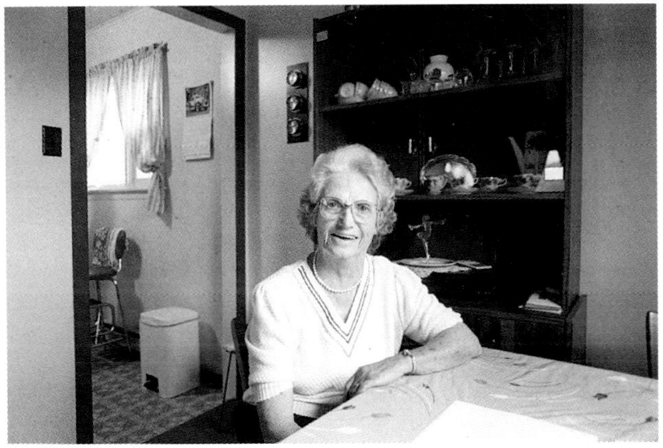

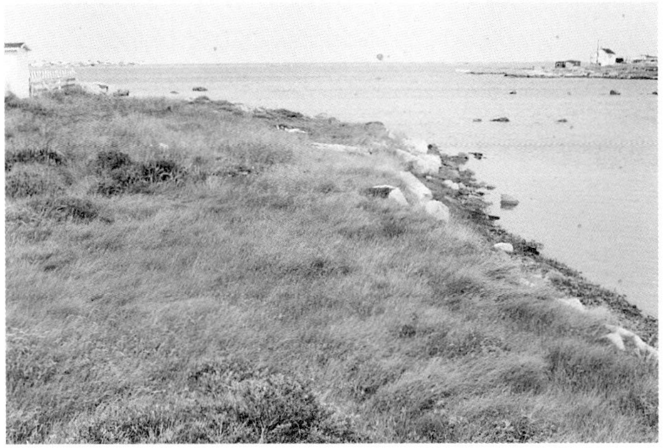

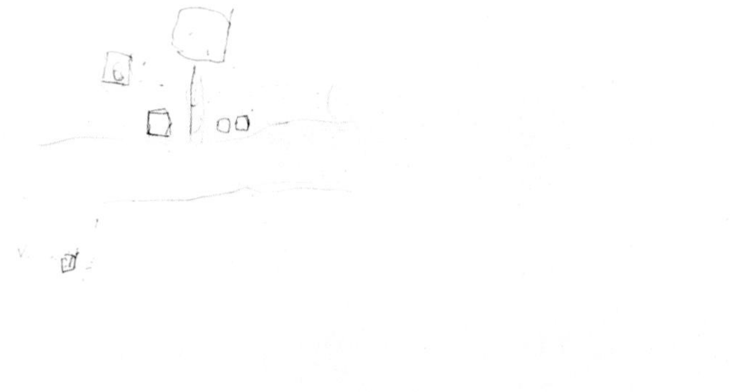

Mabel Eva Leyte *née* Freake

You're down here in the garden, you've got your tent out here somewhere. There's Doug's workshop here. Then, 'tis a little small house. Then the next house is Doug's house. Well, there, that was the Union store. Dad told me that down there was a blacksmith shop. Foxy John Freake, my great-grandfather, was working on this road, the main road, up past this, and people from Tilting came up. And usually there's one person in every place is a strong person, you know. There was Bill Foley from Tilting came along. He was called Big Bill. Dad told me this story, this is why I know. Big Bill told Great-grandfather to move, he wanted to get by. And of course Great-grandfather said no, he was doing repairs to the road. So then Big Bill said, "Do you know who I am? I'm Big Bill Foley." And Great-grandfather said, "Yes, and do you know who I am? I'm Foxy John Freake." And with that he hit him. Put him out like a light, back into the cart. And then the men that were with him hightailed it back to Tilting, they took him back. I gather from when Dad was telling me, it was up there, I'm not sure of the spot. He was known as Foxy John Freake because he had a big long red beard. Strong, he said he was really strong.

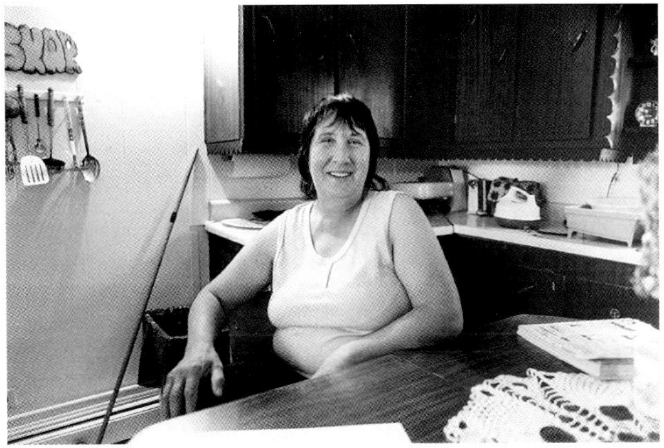

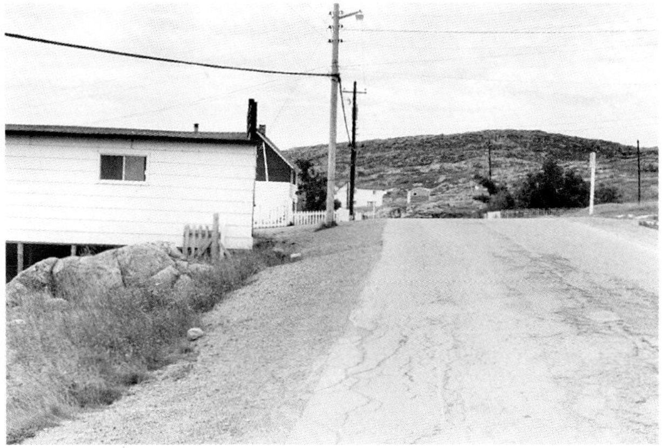

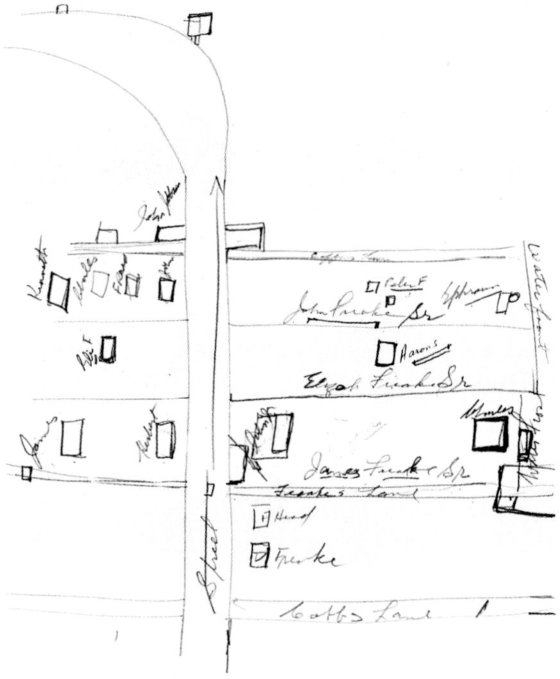

Charlie Freake

Two of the brothers went to Lewisporte, that would be James and Elijah. It was your great-great-grandfather's land, then, that my family inherited. My father, James, is called after your great-great-grandfather. It seems the three brothers were close. We'll begin with the waterfront down here. The strip of land goes down to the waterfront. There's only one house now on that land that's occupied. There used to be five. There's the street there. That was just a cowpath when we were growing up. Here in Elijah's land, Aaron's house is still there. It's not occupied now. James Freake, your great-great-grandfather, I heard his house was launched up in the bottom, right up in the bottom of Joe Batt's Arm. It was a little house. It had meaning for me, I remember it being the home of James Freake.

They used to go up to Lewisporte for the winter. Take the whole family, take the animals too. I know that because I did that as a little boy. Take chickens and pigs and hogs and goats. They had big schooners to go to Lewisporte for the winter. The reason was, they went in there to cut timber for their stages and flakes, and build schooners and punts.

The Freakes came from Christchurch, in Dorsetshire. And when we were there, Lucy and I, both of us growing up in a fisherman's house, when we went down to walk along the waterfront, I don't know who said it to whom, I believe it was Lucy said to me, "Don't you get the feeling you've been here before?"

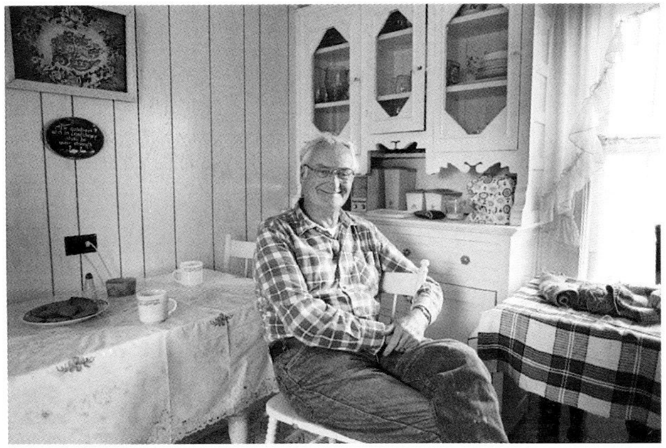

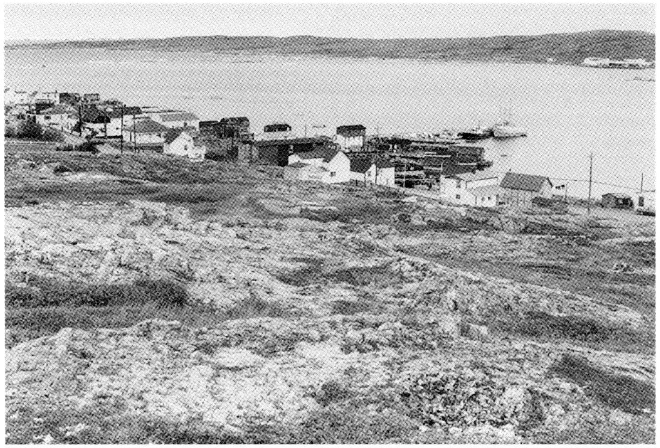

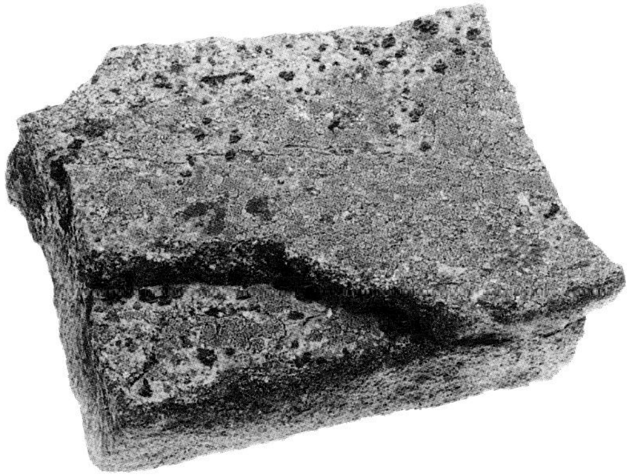

Published in conjunction with an exhibition at Watershed Media Centre, Bristol, England.

Works from the *Places of Presence* series have also been in the following exhibitions:

1992 Dalhousie University Art Gallery, Halifax, Nova Scotia, *Rephotographing the Land*

1992 Moncton, New Brunswick, through Galerie d'art de l'Université de Moncton, *Impact: Public Installations by Artists of Atlantic Canada / Installations publiques par des artistes du Canada atlantique*

1993 La Centrale, Montréal, Québec, *Pièces d'identités*

1993 Gallery 44, Toronto, Ontario, *Marlene Creates: Places of Presence*

1993 Art Gallery of Windsor, Windsor, Ontario, *Margins of Memory*

Marlene Creates: Landworks 1979-1991

1993 Art Gallery of Memorial University, St. John's, Newfoundland, and touring:
Carleton University Art Gallery, Ottawa, Ontario
Southern Alberta Art Gallery, Lethbridge, Alberta

1994 Confederation Centre Art Gallery, Charlottetown, Prince Edward Island
Winnipeg Art Gallery, Winnipeg, Manitoba

1995 Dalhousie University Art Gallery, Halifax, Nova Scotia

1994 Struts Centre, Sackville, New Brunswick, *The Vocation of Storytelling: rooted in community*

1994 Mary March Regional Museum, Grand Falls, Newfoundland, *Marlene Creates: Places of Presence*
Southern Newfoundland Seamen's Museum, Grand Bank, Newfoundland, *Marlene Creates: Places of Presence*

1995 Canadian Museum of Contemporary Photography, Ottawa, *Displaced Histories / Histoires déplacées*

1995 Walter Phillips Gallery, Banff, Alberta, *Storyland: Narrative Vision and Social Space*

1995 La Chambre Blanche, Québec, Québec, *Marlene Creates: Persistance de la géographie*

1997 McMichael Canadian Art Collection, Kleinburg, Ontario, *Marlene Creates: The Colour of My Voice, the Colour of the Land, Newfoundland 1996 and Selected Works*

Marlene Creates lives in St. John's, Newfoundland, Canada. She was born in Montreal in 1952 and studied visual arts at Queen's University in Kingston, Ontario. She lived in Ottawa for twelve years before moving to Newfoundland – the home of her maternal ancestors – in 1985. Since the 1970s her work has been presented in approximately 150 solo and group exhibitions across Canada and in Ireland, Scotland, England, France, Denmark, and the USA. She has also been the curator of several exhibitions, worked in artist-run centres, and taught visual arts at the University of Ottawa and Algonquin College. She has been a guest lecturer at many institutions including the Glasgow School of Art, the University of Oxford, and the University of Kent at Canterbury. Her artistic practice – investigating the relationship between human experience, memory, language and the land – has taken her to work in many locations throughout Canada and Britain. Her work is in numerous public collections including the National Gallery of Canada and the Canadian Museum of Contemporary Photography.